COLORSCAPES

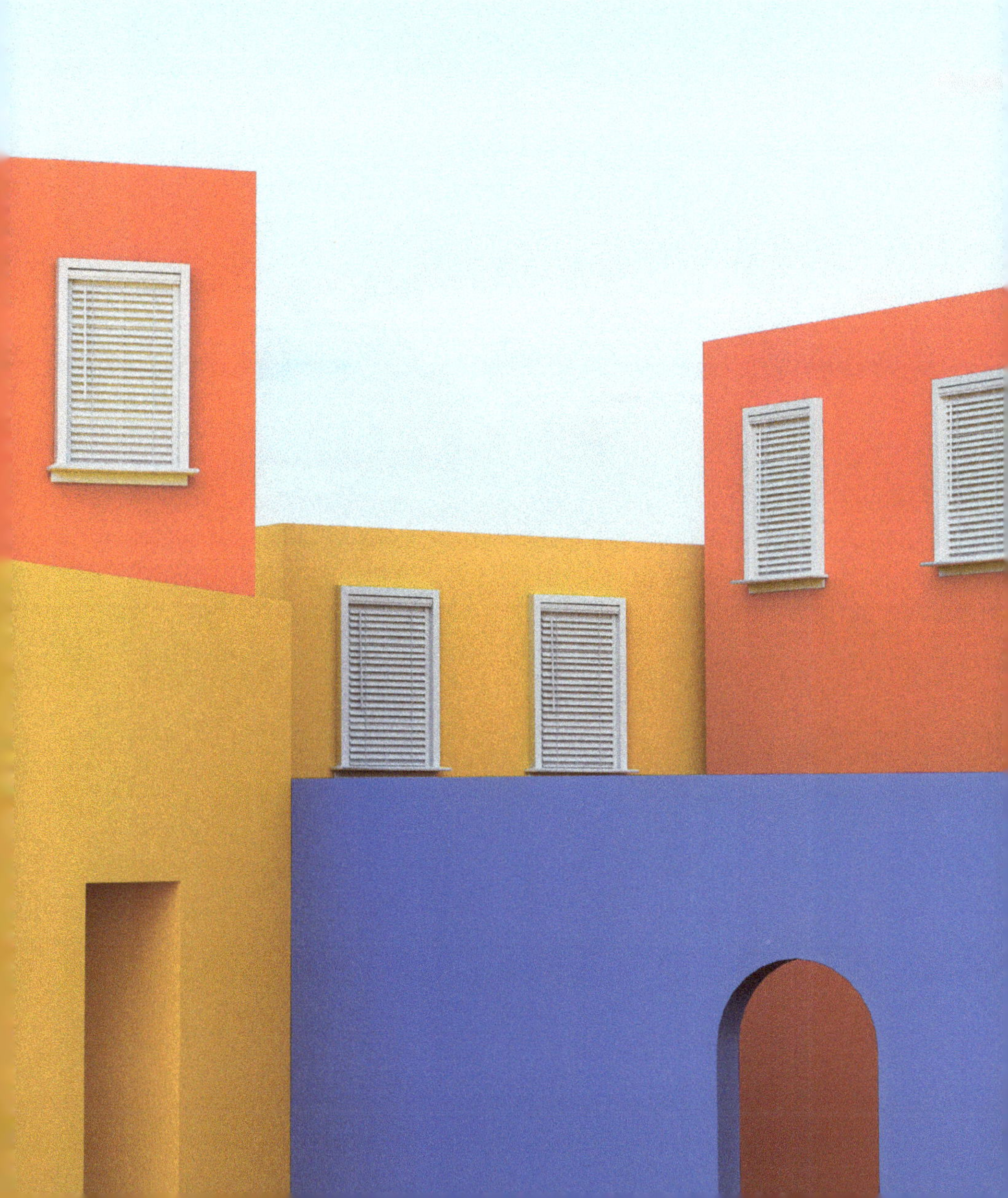

COLORSCAPES

poetry by

LEE WOODMAN

SHANTI ARTS PUBLISHING
BRUNSWICK, MAINE

COLORSCAPES

Published by Shanti Arts Publishing
Designed by Shanti Arts Designs

Cover image by fatih / kgqu_qs3B78 / unsplash.com

Shanti Arts LLC
193 Hillside Road
Brunswick, Maine 04011
shantiarts.com

Printed in the United States of America

ISBN: 978-1-962082-86-0 (softcover)

Library of Congress Control Number: 2025950392

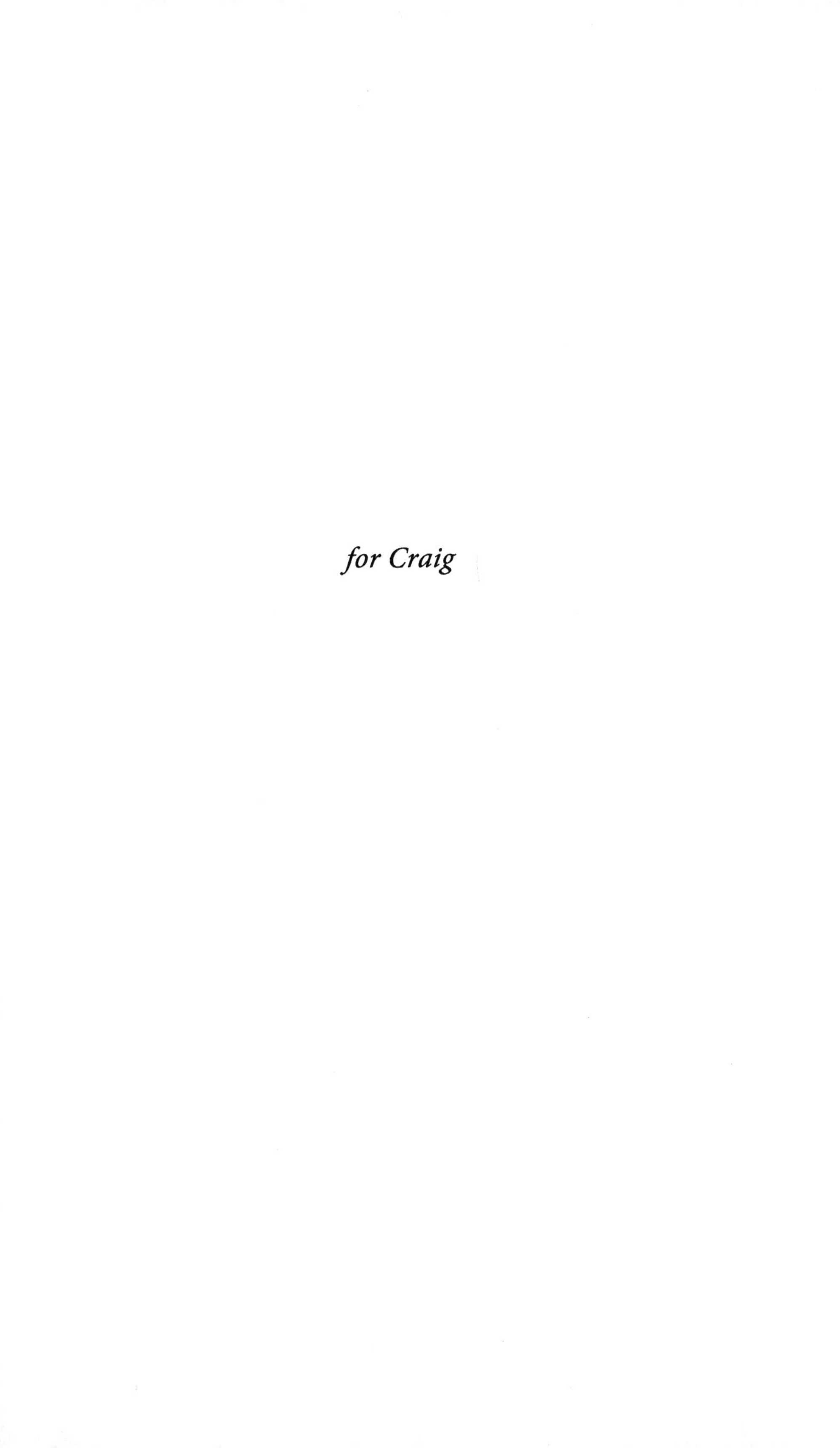

for Craig

CONTENTS

IMAGES

(1)   point-normal / vLSj5Y5LfHY / unsplash.com

(18)   yapo-zhou / YIPSx8PFi9s / unsplash.com

(20)   To view the image that inspired this poem, go to: https://www.anothermag.com/fashion-beauty/3094/leonardo-dicaprio-with-a-swan

(24)   Lee Woodman. Used with permission.

(31)   pawel-czerwinski / 5MPzX_KtL8c / unsplash.com

(33)   Wojciech Kocot, Nepal, 2018. Wikimedia Commons. Creative Commons.

(39)   [top left] Amedeo Modigliani, *Girl in a Green Blouse*, 1917. Oil on canvas. 32 x 18.1 inches (81.3 x 46 cm). National Gallery of Art, Washington, D.C. Wikimedia Commons. Public Domain.

[top middle] Richard Bergh, *Portrait of Gerda* (Gerda Ingeborg Winkrans), 1895. Oil on canvas. 58.8 x 36 inches (149.5 x 91.5 cm). National Museum of Art, Architecture and Design, Oslo, Norway. Wikimedia Commons. Public Domain.

[top right] Sarah Shewell Hayden, *Girl in Green (The Green Gown)*, 1899. Oil on canvas. 35 x 26 inches (88.9 x 66 cm). Sheldon Museum of Art, Lincoln, Nebraska. Wikimedia Commons. Public Domain.

[bottom left] Boris Grigoriev, *Portrait of a Young Woman in a Green Dress*, 1926. Oil on canvas. 28.4 x 21.2 inches (72.2 x 54 cm). Private Collection. Wikimedia Commons. Public Domain.

[bottom right] Felix Nussbaum, *Self-portrait with Green Hat*. Wikimedia Commons. Public Domain.

(44)   Lee Woodman. Used with permission.

(47)   wolfgang-hasselmann / TnN8puomHx4 / unsplash.com

(53)   dustin-humes / IkYpVrXx4y8 / unsplash.com

(57)   alex-shuper / cPyaklYL51Q / unsplash.com

(59)   neven-krcmarek / 6smgFbwHm_4 / unsplash.com

(62)   wolfgang-hasselmann / y9On4Mjp12M / unsplash.com

(65)   eugene-golovesov / aeQuBhhSfwE / unsplash.com

(69)   Lee Woodman. Used with permission.

(73) a-chosen-soul / 4GGRCPBXyrI / unsplash.com

(75) a-chosen-soul / jXsVdC3Eyag / unsplash.com

(76) Kuba-Dis, Comparison of RGB and CMYK color models, 2011. Wikimedia Commons. Public Domain.

(80) content-pixie / 14Xl_B4Apk4 / unsplash.jpg

(87) amir-esrafili / X8Cao0DbiDg / unsplash.jpg

(89) rosie-kerr / ZgM7nVYJ9GA / unsplash.jpg

(90) charlee / H48ivodYpS8 / unsplash.jpg

(93) alksndra / tZ-oOlzwiQI / unsplash.jpg

(96) fons-heijnsbroek / F7X0wBAgB4o / unsplash.jpg

(97) fons-heijnsbroek / QnnXlHZFHpU / unsplash.jpg

(101) Lee Woodman, #7 Lotus Pond. Used with permission.

(105) Lee Woodman. Used with permission.

(108) To view the image that inspired this poem, go to: https://www.nga.gov/collection/art-object-page.60.html

(109) ehsan-ahmadnejad / l8Bxmy0Qux4 / unsplash.com

(111) Wassily Kandinsky, *Improvisation 31 (Sea Battle)*, 1913. Oil on canvas. 55.3 x 47.1 inches (140.7 x 119.7 cm). National Gallery of Art, Washington, D. C. Wikimedia Commons. Public Domain.

(112) To view the image that inspired this poem, go to: https://www.thedavidhockneyfoundation.org/chronology/1972

(115) angus-gray / qEaELLSYZW0 / unsplash.com

(117) To view the image that inspired this poem, go to: https://collection.carnegieart.org/objects/51619113-31b2-4418-9d63-6ef4767882ee

(120) Caravaggio, *The Beheading of St. John the Baptist*, 1608. Oil on canvas. 11.8 x 17 feet (361 x 520 cm). St. John's Co-Cathedral, Valletta, Malta. Wikimedia Commons. Public Domain.

(123) [top] Antonio_AI / 1263076906 / stock.adobe.com [bottom] Gzvzattio_AI / 1491850584 / stock.adobe.com

(128) pawel-czerwinski / kmlIF2QRwx0 / unsplash.com; content-pixie / kAkmmMwNIJo / unsplash.com

(131) To view the image that inspired this poem, go to: https://www.arthistoryproject.com/artists/hilma-af-klint/group-ix-uw-no-25-the-dove-no-1/

(135) william-warby / l525sUeY4Ss / unsplash.com

Acknowledgments

The author extends her gratitude to the publishers of the following books in which these poems previously appeared:

ARTSCAPES (Shanti Arts Publishing, 2022)
　"Yves Blue"

HOMESCAPES (Finishing Line Press, 2020)
　"Ruby Necklace"
　"Snowporch"
　"Two Crickets, Two Bees, and a Hydrangea"

LIFESCAPES (Kelsay Books 2021)
　"Castles in the Air"

MINDSCAPES (Poets Choice Publishing 2020)
　"My Dinner with Athena"
　"Rebirth on the Quay"
　"Yellow into Yellow"

SOULSCAPES (Shanti Arts Publishing, 2023)
　"Farewell to Glorious Pink at the Basin"
　"Serenity Hues"
　"Shades of Anger"
　"Tints of Anguish"

Thanks ...

I am grateful to the people who made this book possible ...

... my sister and first reader, novelist Betsy Woodman, who makes life brighter and keeps me laughing;

... my master poets, critics, and publishers: Virginia Mecklenburg, Margaret Hasse, Emily Holland, Zeina Azzam, Grace Cavalieri, Sue Ellen Thompson, Richard Blanco, Alexandra Oliver, Lorette Luzajic, Jane Rosenberg Laforge, Sparrow, Richard Harteis, Leah Maines, Karen Kelsay, Claudia Gary, and Christine Cote;

... writers from the priceless Monday group, who kindly welcomed a poet among novelists: Elizabeth Berg, Mary Mitchell, Donna Stein, and Betsy Woodman;

... my steadfast colleague and archivist, Bill Kircher; IT guru, Mustafa Bahar; marketing coach, Brian Feinblum; and editor, Sarah Jewell;

... my cherished friends and supporters: Craig Kraft, Virginia Rice, Sarah Toth, Randy Wynn, Julianna Jacobson, Pete Chauvette, Susan Clampitt, Jeremy Waletzky, Madeleine Jacobs, and Marjorie Share;

... the talented women who made reading and writing so healing during the pandemic and will do so into the future: Dawn Raffel, Jill Smolowe, Jane Rosenberg Laforge, Donna Stein, Betsy Woodman, Laura Weiss, Ronna Weinberg, Pamela Walker, and Ellen Prentiss Campbell;

. . . the magical visionaries at the Writer's Hotel and *The New Guard Literary Review:* founding editor, Shanna McNair; and consulting editor, Scott Wolven;

. . . and to inspirational books on color: *Color, A Master Class*, Camille Viéville; *The Secret Lives of Color*, Kassia St. Clair; *Colors of Art*, Chloë Ashby, *Theory of Colors*, Johann Wolfgang von Goethe; and *Interaction of Color*, Josef Albers.

PREFACE

"Colors are words' little sisters . . . I've loved them secretly for a long time."

> —Rolf Jacobsen

My life has been drenched in color, one joyful splash after another. As a kid in India, I absorbed the rich oranges and red spices in the marketplace and the wild combos of yellows, greens, and purples in women's saris. In the spring festival of Holi, I got smeared with bright blues and pinks, and the smells are still in my nostrils.

College studies in European and American art history introduced me to color theory and the phenomenology of perception. I took many studio courses—painting, silk screen, graphic design, ceramics—and broadened my art horizons during a year at the University of Paris's l'Institut d'Art et d'Archéologie and the Louvre. I was so excited, I could hardly sleep!

Then came a career at the Smithsonian, the Library of Congress, and other wonderful stewards of art, architecture, technology, and science. So many opportunities to submerge myself in color. Think of *The Eclipse*, by artist Alma Thomas, 1970—wild concentric bands of yellow, red, and blue stripes.

Color in nature and the laboratory continues to fascinate me. Where do different dyes come from— shells, rocks, insects, chemicals? What did artists Josef and Anni Albers teach us bout color relationships? And what do psychologists and philosophers from

Goethe to Isaac Newton to Carl Jung tell us about color perception for human beings?

Why is a particular music style called the Blues? The red of Coca-Cola a closely-guarded trade secret? The turtleneck in a catalog sold as sea-foam-green one year and mysterious-mint the next? What does your favorite color make you feel? What is chiaroscuro, anyway? Join me on a journey to talk about, revel in, and see color in a brand new light.

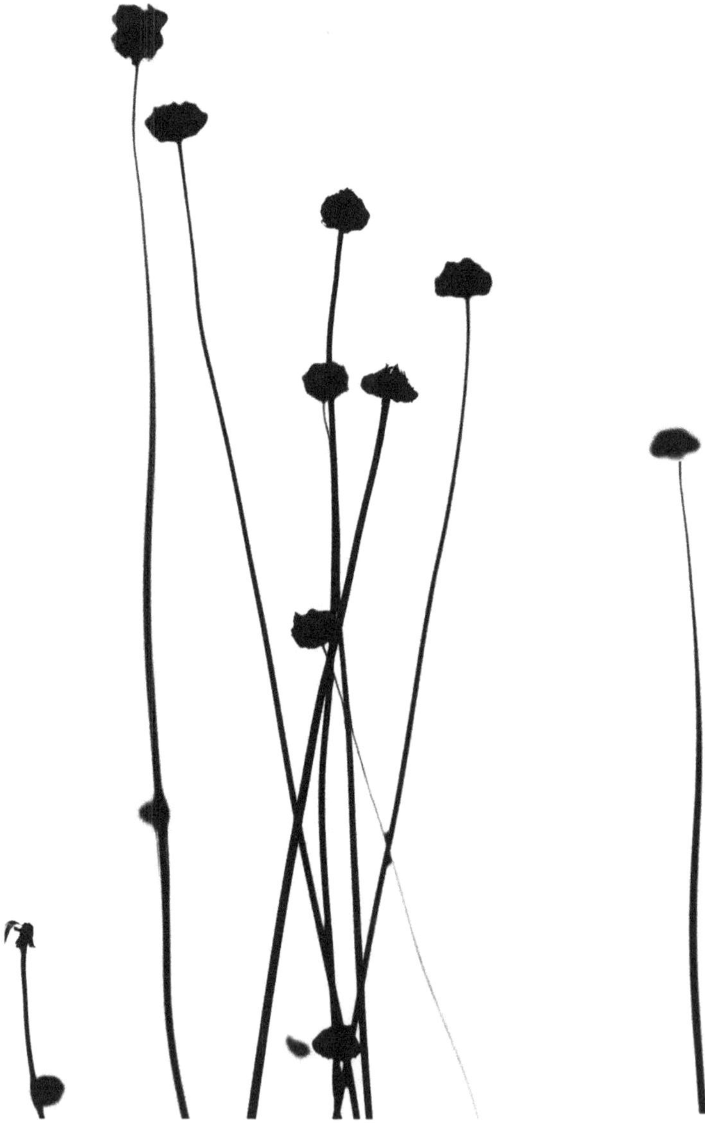

18

Black Is Not a Color

Just an absence of light . . .

Churchill's "black dog" crushed Kenyon and Plath,
slogging the towpath, dreading the warpath

John Donne quizzed his soul for blackness of sin,
knowing life was full of menace—his fears within

echoed voices of doom—the blare of Hell
where whiffs of death lingered, waited for mortals

Naked and black, goddess Kali was monstrous—
her necklace of skulls, her temper so reckless

Bubonic Black Death killed soldiers and civilians,
bacteria from rats and fleas decimated millions

Creepy black creatures connected to Satan—
crows, bats and cats—the mind's cruel creation

Whether charcoal, or jet, or ink or obsidian,
black presents conflicting complications—

the richness of velvet, the pinnacle of fashion,
yet shadows of black conjure witches, assassins

The plight of psychosis, a terror so visceral,
the soaked sheets of midnight bring panic attacks,

a daily helping of death—pure pitch black

Leonardo DiCaprio with a Swan

—inspired by Annie Leibovitz, a contemporary practitioner of
chiaroscuro, and her photos of celebrities in the 60s, 70s, 80s

Looking back at your photos of famous stars,
    drama in black and white—
    John and Yoko, Leonardo

I remember boomer times,
    when our boyfriends wore long
    hair and peace symbols

and we got jobs, went braless,
    and vied for equal pay. You
    showed us light and dark—

a paler John in fetus pose,
    clinging to darker Yoko,
    black hair fanned wide on the rug

Hollywood sensation DiCaprio, with his
        boy-band hair flecked stone gray,
        crouched in slightly-lit cattails,

hugging a zinc-white swan, her neck
        draped around his ultra-vantablack
        turtleneck. Intimate and sinister—

Settings of significance, personal traits
        and poses—you captured their
        quirks with a wide-angle lens

Cast shadows, reflected light, streaks
        of mystery, timeless portraits,
        contrasts we can't forget—

Chiaroscuro

SHELLS AND ROCKS

Eighty million years ago, I died.

Call me Coccolithophores for that's what I was and what I am

Once a mammofossil—the soft milk of marine ooze—

over epochs, became a compounded shell,

compacted with teeny microscopic plankton friends.

I became bedrock on the ocean floor,

pushed skyward to become the White Cliffs of Dover.

What a gift to be revived from such depths—

Imagine me,

sea algae in calcite, now building blocks of towering heights.

Imagine me,

being quarried, washed in water, left to settle

in large vats to separate my many layers.

I love the tales of artists over millennia choosing

the strata they seek—

the top band drained to be the finest are

Chinese White oils, gouache and water color.

The bottom rung, the coarsest—whitewash.

A lifetime of decomposition—pounded, left to solidify,

I am reduction itself.

Reincarnated both below water and above ground,

fluids pass through me—I am rock, I am color.

I am chalk.

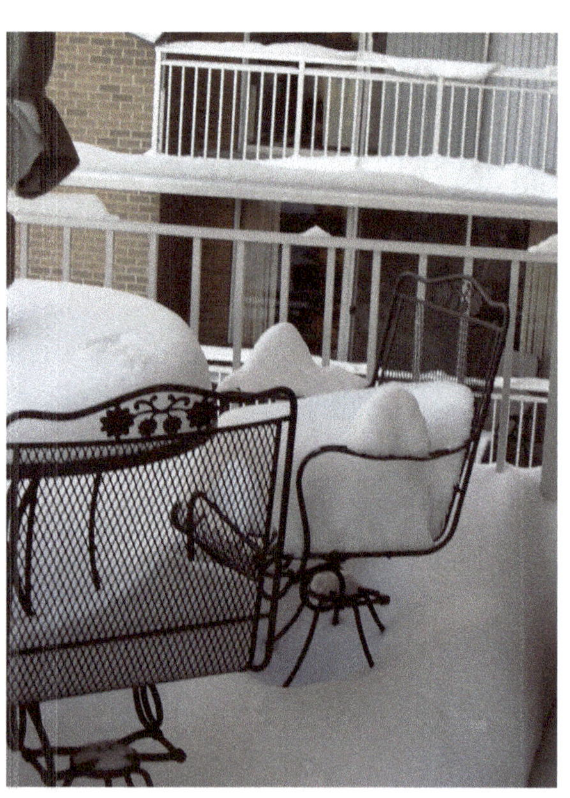

SNOWPORCH

Snow piled up Sunday
swirling on the balcony
Two wrought iron chairs
braced for the season snuggle
cloaked with puffy white armrests

TOWARD BIG SUR

It used to be about the sea,
       now earth and sky loom large

Down the seductive highway,
       the massive clouds take charge

Misting moist, careening,
       they come as one white swarm

of conquering troops to cover,
       the towering cliffs transform

Fronds of foxtails lean skyward
       backlit near the ground,

fighting the invasion that
       masks the sun they found

So windy, ardent, windy,
       the sheet of white advances,

grass and red rash ground bushes
       hold on tight to baldness

A blow of scent from soybean fields,
     strong smell of cauliflower,

battles hard with sweet incense
        from furrowed bark of cedar

From brazen spruce emollients,
        pungent perfume lances

Soon the rays will burn the cloud
        changing the advantage

Nothing stays the way it was,
        the victor always alters,

at first the sun, and then the wind
        and then great clouds take over

Gray ocean pounds away below,
        as chorus for the warfare

Yves Blue

*—after Yves Klein's Untitled Blue Sponge Relief, 1960,
Glenstone Museum, Potomac, Maryland*

Surrender to the mystery,

experience the relentless hue—

let your limbs go limp,

bathe in abstract obsession

of Blue Revolution,

succumb to the Klein void.

The voices of his sponges

cry vertiginous blue—

Sheer monochromes of

aerated pumice, haute-relief,

turn away from

oppressive steel-gray,

refuse the foul-brown of earth.

Impossible to make his color

behave, don't even try—

float in the pocket of his sea,

wade in magic waters,

lift the arch of your foot.

Yield, or the enormity

will inseminate, impregnate,

crush you like a macaroon,

roll you like an airless puck.

Weighted bubbles of blue can

fall to the base of the canvas,

sometimes fly vertical or horizontal.

Loaded pigment does not leak—

Yves' Ultramarine.

Utopia of unruly blue!

A Scold of Blue Jays

Down, down, barely skimming the slate rock hillside,
        jeering as finches scatter,
                the alpha jay lands on the river birch

Within seconds, screaming blue streams of followers
        dive through spindly branches of the tree,
                brazen winds have stripped all its leaves

Only long enough to perch and rebound, the roil of birds
        merge, swerving back up to the top of the hill
                A woodpecker freezes

Screeching surrounds a wobbling nest,
        too heavy for the scant limbs of a red oak,
                the day roost of a saw-whet owl

The mottled brown bird waits, trembling,
        then hurtles into nearby bronzing oaks
                still wearing cloaks of dry leaves

The adolescent pack redoubles its game,
        darting downward toward the river birch,
                readying to reverse again, another charge

The big jay stays behind, content to claim
        a solo perch nearby. The woodpecker and owl
                eye his necklace of black, pale blue breast,

while the ringleader goes through his repertoire
        soto voce—clicks, rattles, mews, peeps,
                queedles,

Jeers

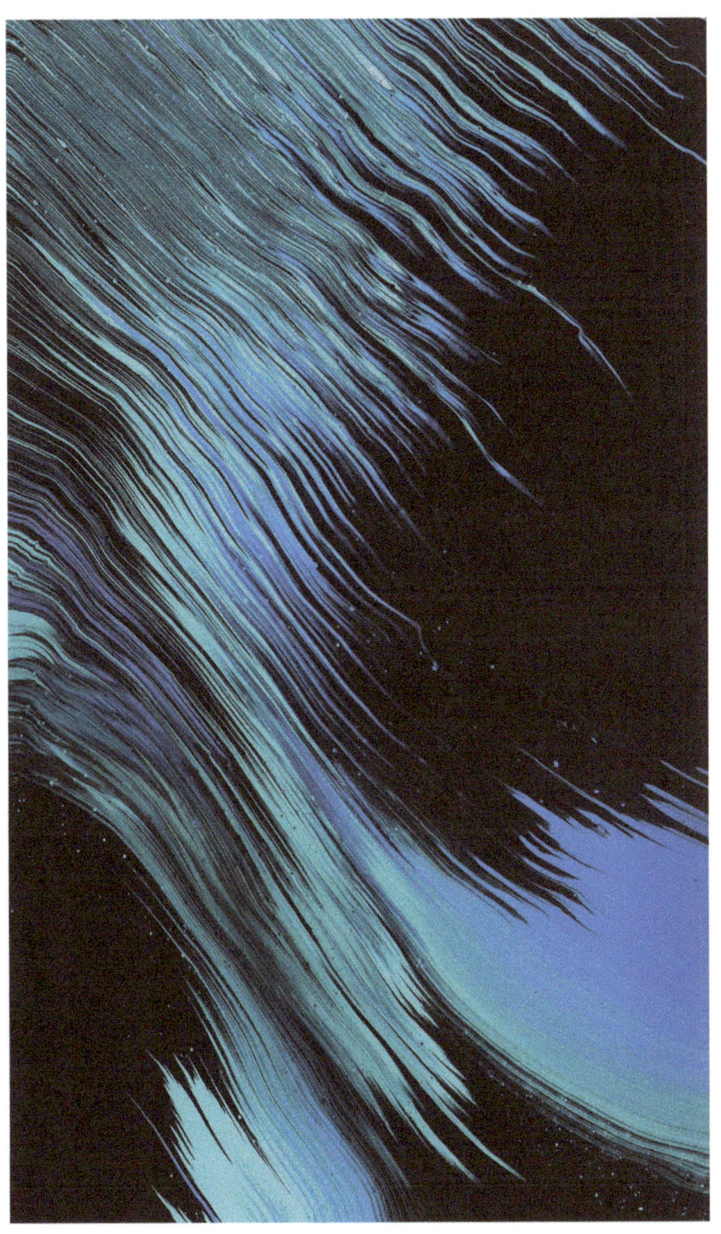

TURQUOISE DHARMA

Jeti's prayer wheel and handle are turquoise,

a lively greenish-blue with a filigree design,

embedded with reddish-golden coral studs.

Jeti climbs the rocky gorge,

following a queue of other Nepalese devotees—

> *Om Mani Padme Hum,*
> *Om Mani Padme Hum*

Her chant is silent, like theirs, but the mountains listen,

the monasteries hear.

> *Om Mani Padme Hum,*
> *Om Mani Padme Hum*

Each pilgrim holds a prayer wheel, a cylindrical sheetmetal body,

mounted on a shaft, set into a wooden handle.

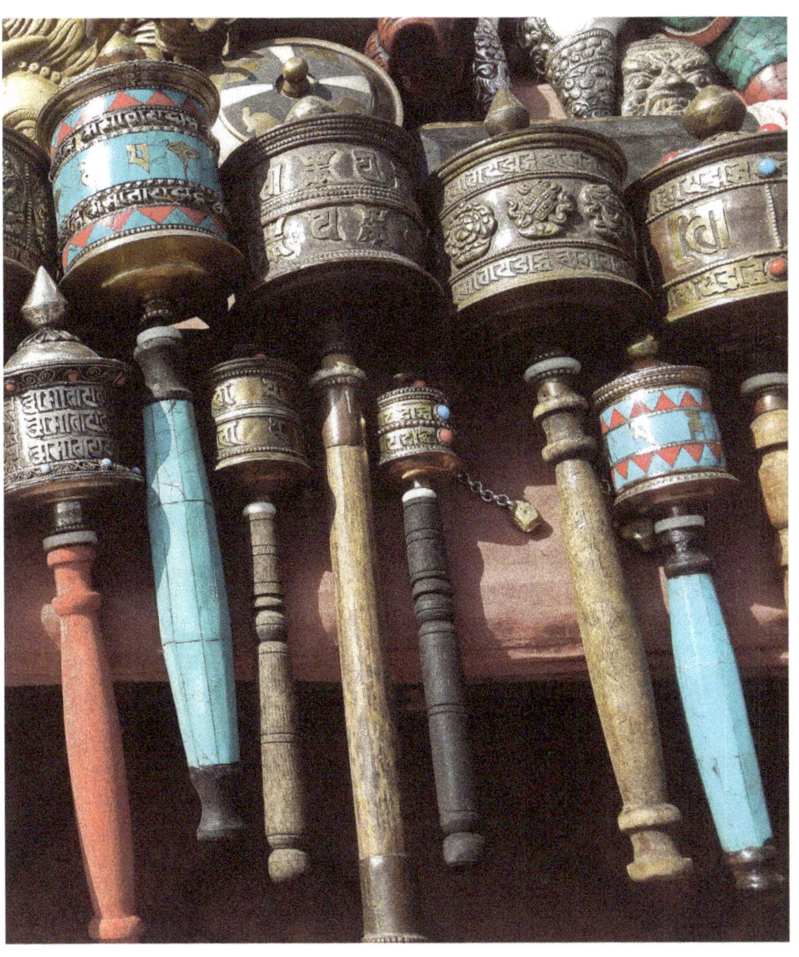

On the cylinders are small chains with weighted beads
     on the end,

helping to keep the wheels in orbit.

On the outside of each wheel, the mantra is welded in Sanskrit—

   Om Mani Padme Hum

On the inside, a long strip of rolled-up tissue paper,

repeats the phrase in ink, thousands of times.

Tibetans call turquoise "Sky Tone," a protector and token of love.

Higher and higher the climbers mount, toward the blue,

intent on spreading goodwill to all sentient beings.

Rocks tumble across the pilgrims' path, but they are surefooted,

focused on accumulating wisdom, building merit.

The marchers gaze up at two-hundred-year-old larches,

and breathe in the scent of spruce and fir.

Snow lions, celestial animals, have been watching,

waiting in the cold stillness for muffled chants.

The atmosphere thins, a richness of nothingness—

the bringers of good fortune proceed forward,

wafting incense drifts down from the nearby monastery.

The practitioners redouble

reeling of wheels—

Jeti whirls hers clockwise in a gentle rhythm,

releasing thousands of mantras . . . more than she could ever speak

in a fraction of the time.

A silent zephyr blows words and purification aloft:

Om Mani Padme Hum,
Om Mani Padme Hum

Om Mani Padme Hum,
Om Mani Padme Hum

Secret Life of a Porcelain Pot

A delicate blue vase, shaped like clapping scallop shells,
sits on a pearl saucer with pie-crust curves.

A closer look shows the sides are flat strips of clay—
the gentle blue appears soft to the eye, but rough to the touch.

Small bits of porcelain chips flare out all around—
tiny green leaves, blue-and-white spiral dots,

mini yellow daisies. All fragile, but frozen in place
because the vase was fired in blinding heat.

But wait. This stable silent object, earnest in its splendor,
holds more. Human words to describe it only know so much.

Turned sideways, it has a secret life, moves with ease,
living a fantasy of its own. When no one is near,

it takes off like a tropical fish into magical waters,
propelled by its tiny buds and leaves as fins,

angling through corals to join millions of shoal-mates,
advancing and reversing, flipping and darting.

All swim in waves of fluidity and vanishing color—
cherry, orange, emerald. Delicate blue with dots.

When Ashbery Invites O'Hara Chez Moi

John proposes a plan to his cherished friend Frank—
I know you planned tonight at The Five Spot,
but we could meet for drinks at Bowery Poetry?
Or, how about a slightly different plan?
A friend of mine lives the next block over,
she's ethereal, wildly weird, and cooks curry.
Former dancer, now she's into theater,
you know the syzygy of art, music, dance.
I'm pretty sure you'll see things eye to eye—
her place is bohème, she drives a beater,
and hangs odd-shaped mirrors everywhere.
You can wear velour, for sure—your emerald vest,
she'll be braless in a muumuu.
We have a lot to finish with our poems
we started together—
maybe even add rhyme?
"I like your poem, now the violets are gone,"
meanwhile, musicians will be working on their scores.
The folks at MOMA may be in a flurry,
because your exhibits raise the stakes,
but please take a break. Come where
folks are much more hybrid,
bring along your scotch and typewriter.
Lilly will stir some aloo saag and vindaloo,
break out with some crooning.
We'll have a hoot with our best pals,
playing jazz on her untuned piano.
She may climb on the table, dance,
or stand on our shoulders,
hoping to find her balance over time.

The Many Faces of Green

"Absolute green is the most anesthetizing color
possible . . . similar to a fat cow, lying down,
contemplating the world through stupid
inexpressive eyes." —Wassily Kandinsky

Green may have an image problem—
Like naïve youth considered green,
or arsenic found in Scheele green, or
bluish copper carbonate called verdigris

When alchemists mixed elements,
foxglove and nettle only produced dim green
When Edgar Allen Poe devoured absinthe—
the "Green Fairy," was thought to be deadly

Yet, picture the glory of being green,
imagine three hundred shades in nature—
olive, pine, apple green, and moss,
laurel, kelp, mantis, and sap

Take in tender shoots of spring,
rejoice when forest-greens leaf out in June,
celebrate the undulating green moray eel,
the lime green luna moth, the virid spider

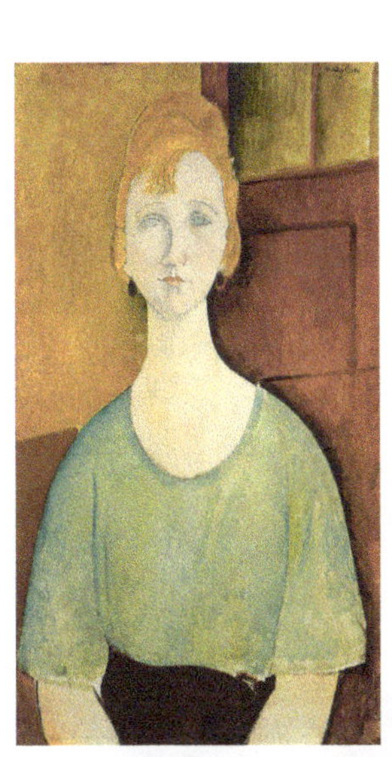

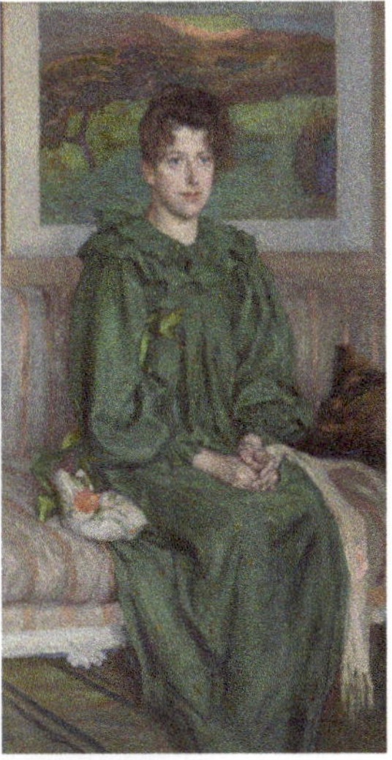

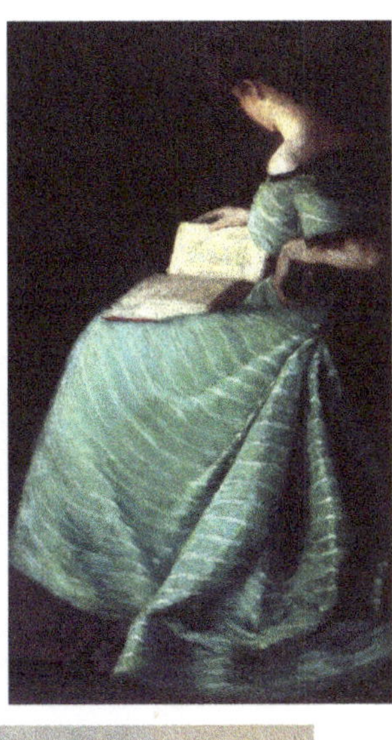

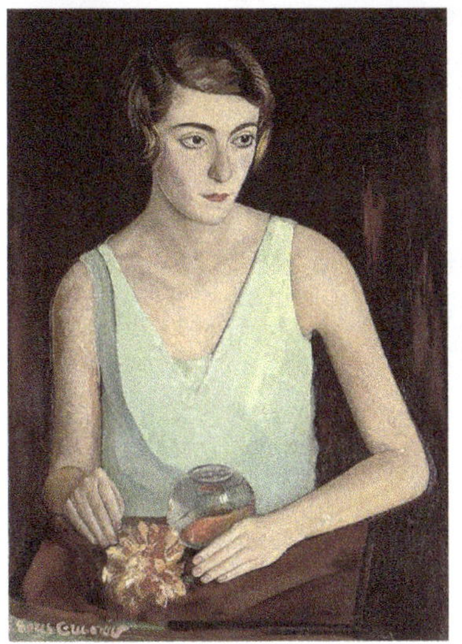

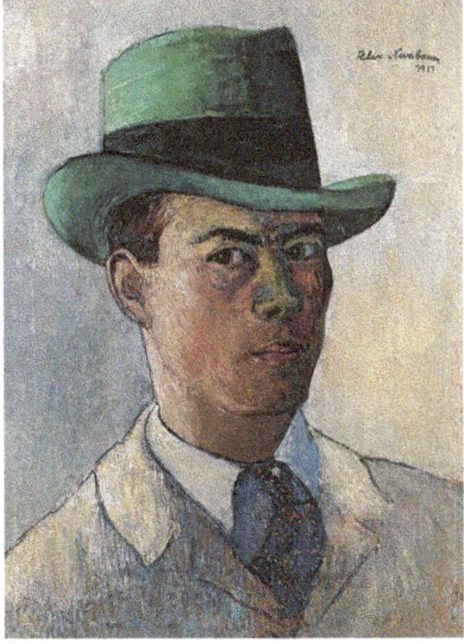

Be proud of creating a nutritious salad—
toss up cabbage, kale, spinach, and watercress,
greenhouse celery, cucumbers, green peppers
Chomp into bitter arugula and watery romaine

Lie down in a verdant garden to savor sweet scents,
speak to *Eucalyptus* trees who will lessen depression
Gallop over the mead and paddock,
wear your shamrock on St Paddy's Day

Delight in Kermit's words, "It's not easy being Green,"
and sound out the smorgasbord of alluring hues—
evergreen, emerald, kelly, and malachite,
celadon, Terre Verte, avocado, and pickle

Feast your eyes on Van Eyck's bottle-green dress
in *Arnolfini's Portrait.* Marvel at how Seurat
pointillated patches of dotty green pigments
in *Sunday Afternoon on Island of La Grande Jatte*

And, despite how Kandinsky threw down the gauntlet,
peek to see how *he* punctuated with splotches
of absolute green to make his red and blue colors pop—
hardly anesthetic, especially in the eye of a cow

DEVIL WITH MY GREEN DRESS ON

—inspired by Mitch Ryder and the Detroit Wheels' song
"Devil with a Blue Dress"

Deep green emerald dress,
    most expensive ever bought

Velvet, low V-neck, fitted at waist,
    knee-length bell-shaped skirt

Tailor at Saks tucks the bodice,
    adjusts shoulder seams

Ready for pick-up after Christmas
    to wear for February Opera

Crazy dream blooms up one night,
    Red-haired She-devil declares

"My mother altered your dress.
    It fits me perfectly!

May I wear it to my wedding?
    We are so poor."

Strange dream, strange request,
    I laugh upon waking . . .

When I pick up the dress,
        the tailor is not there

but the dress is ready, zipped
        into the classy Saks bag

Doesn't occur to me to open it
        before the Opera date

Oh the Devil! I open the bag.
        Unmistakable smell of B.O.

She boogied in my dress,
        sweated powerful odors

and rewrapped the fucking bag
        I don't wear it to the Opera

Off I go to Parkway Cleaners,
        reputably the most adept

for furs, leathers, velvets,
    vouched for by Angie's List

Costs as much as the dress price,
    "We clean each inch by hand."

Turandot is wonderful, the dress gorgeous
    amplified by my ruby necklace

Damn, if The Red Devil doesn't show up in
    more wild dreams that night

This time, she only says one thing,
    "Maid of Honor made me do it."

Maid of Honor in the blue dress, blue dress,
    demanded Devil keep my green dress on

44

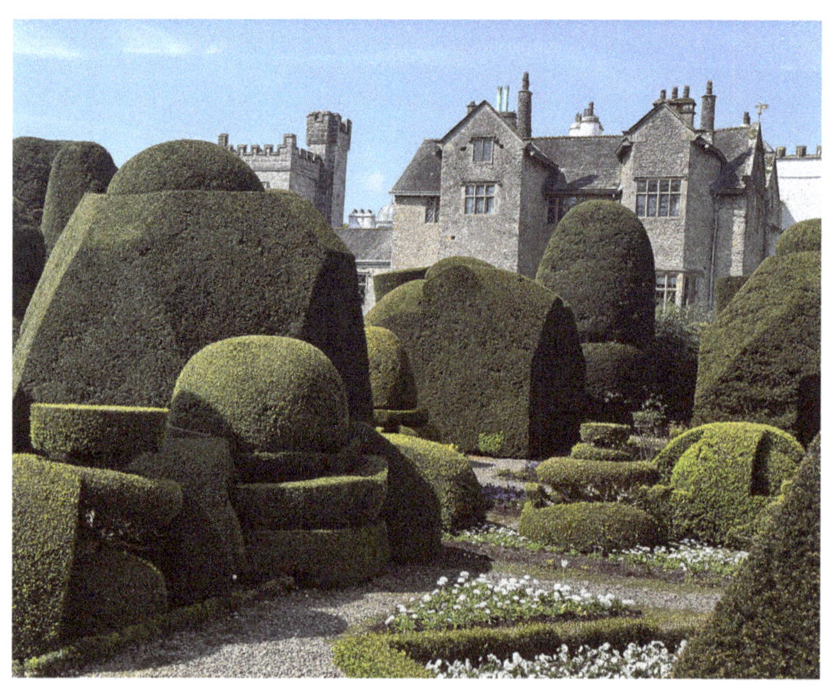

SLUGS, BUGS, AND BUNNIES

—a ballad inspired by a visit to Levens Hall in Cumbria,
England, known for the world's oldest topiary gardens

Boxwoods, privets, and yew prevail
    despite all the creatures that gnaw them
Topiaries galore in all manners of green
    are tended by growers who love them

Spirals, bells, and cubes with cut-outs,
    expertly pruned to stay stable
Carefully seeded centuries ago
    by gardeners known to be able

They know the needs of the trees year-round,
    those that like more shade or sun
The various greens change with the daylight,
    from lime, to artichoke to citron

Chris Crowder, Head Gardener, made an apiary
    near the topiary—tends his own bee garden
Puts jars of honey on an overturned basket
    with a sign that announces a bargain

"A quid for a jar, leave your coin in this pot,"
    (a small terracotta for starters)
What would he grow in the long rows beyond
    but bee balm—cranberry monarda

When asked about threats to acres of gardens,
    he mentions slugs, aphids, and rabbits
Powerful odors can deter the herbivores,
    they don't like ginger or garlic

Slugs and snails tackle tree bark and flowers
    and may well sample the honey
They favor decaying waste from the plants,
    and are not picky eaters, like bunnies

Purple Passion Persists

"It pisses God off if you don't notice purple;
it's a sin not to appreciate beauty in the field."
So says Shug Avery in the film *Color Purple*.

She's thinking of blooms—salvia, sweet pea,
alyssum and petunias. Or, the brightly
colored heliotrope flower. Eye catching.

Ear popping. Metaphor insinuating.
*"Purple Rain, Purple People Eater,
Light in the loafers, Lavender*

*Purple Rage, Purple prose, Purple
Hat Ladies, Born in the Purple, Purple
Haze, The Purple Rose of Cairo"*

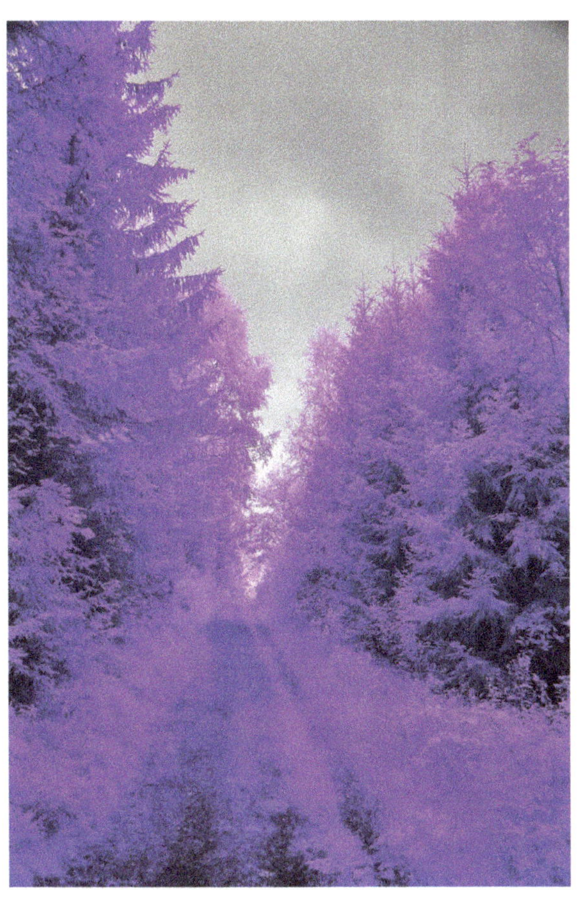

Clothiers, chemists, and artists search
for special purples, dear and deeply hidden,
some from above ground, others below.

From the earth, a plant—a duet of alga
and fungus—is ground to make archil,
a red-purple dye—worn in wool and silk capes.

Tyrian Purple, wrought from sea snails,
results in an even deeper color of royalty,
which nobles bought for eye-watering prices.

The color came from milked sea snails,
at two hundred thousand drops an ounce—
a shining surprise from a dark internal place.

Synthetic dyes like aniline, formed from sticky tar
mixed with tin chloride emerged lighter—
a rich fuchsia hue. *It* was spun to make quinine,

a quirky experiment hoped to cure malaria.
Instead, it turned into a beloved mauve dye,
which Queen Victoria favored, it matched her eyes.

Color meanings alter—from dark and shadowy,
to shiny and gleaming. Painters reveled outdoors,
light ricocheted over the landscapes.

Impressionists mastered bluish-violet tones,
Manet thought the color of atmosphere was violet—
shadows didn't have to be only black or gray.

Critics called the painters "Violettomaniacs,"
Degas, Monet, Cézanne and Pissarro persisted,
using bright complementary colors as shadows.

Delighting in new ways of looking, they daubed on
yellow, green and violet-blue, no more black or gray.
Grass went beyond green, sky invited more than blue—

And, yes, the passion for violet, lavender, and plum,
magenta, mauve, and heliotrope rages on—in clothes,
songs, insults, movies—remember what Shug said,

"It pisses God off if you don't notice purples."

PROVOCATIVE PINK

Like foods that go in and out of favor, so goes color—

coffee, once bad for you, then good, now questionable,

pink has also gone through many reversals.

As early as 1893, pink was for boys. Why?

It was deemed a stronger color than blue—

girls were too dainty and delicate for pink.

Eggs, first high-cholesterol killers, are now thought

to be effective high-protein (especially the whites)

Puce, a whitish shade of pink, was exploited

by Marie Antoinette. King Louis XVI hated

"the color of fleas." He also hated her. Still,

ladies in court swooned in adoration of their queen,

and mimicked the puce of her gowns.

Pepto-Bismol Pink was recommended by shrinks

as a soothing room-color for traumatized patients.

Mountbatten Pink, a lavender gray shade,

was seen as the best camouflage for steamer funnels

in WWI. They got hidden in the gloaming.

Maxi skirts were popular in the Mod 60s and Grunge 90s,

minis rose above the knees in the 60s.

When pop artists designed album covers in the 60s,

pink turned bright and glowing. When Crayola

manufactured pink highlighters, plain text

turned attention-grabbing.

Oh, how we change our hair from braids, to bobs,

to bangs; how we switch from flares, to leggings,

to capris. Yes, we yearn for novelty.

And, for the last word on provocative pinks—

Baker-Miller Pink, Shocking Pink, Fuchsia,

Fluorescent—when it comes to flowers,

the dernier cri is Amaranth, ranging

from cherry red, to dusty grape, to rich plum.

All varieties of *pink* roses turn *green* with envy.

Oranja Glad?

At one point, there was no acknowledged orange—

just yellow-red or red-yellow,

until there came the fruit from China—

naranj, naraga, orange, and the rest began:

William, Prince of Orange

Orangemen from Protestant Ireland

Traffic signs signaling danger

Signature luxury brand Hermès

Prince Harry, the Ginger

Agent Orange, the killer

The tints and shades claimed other names—

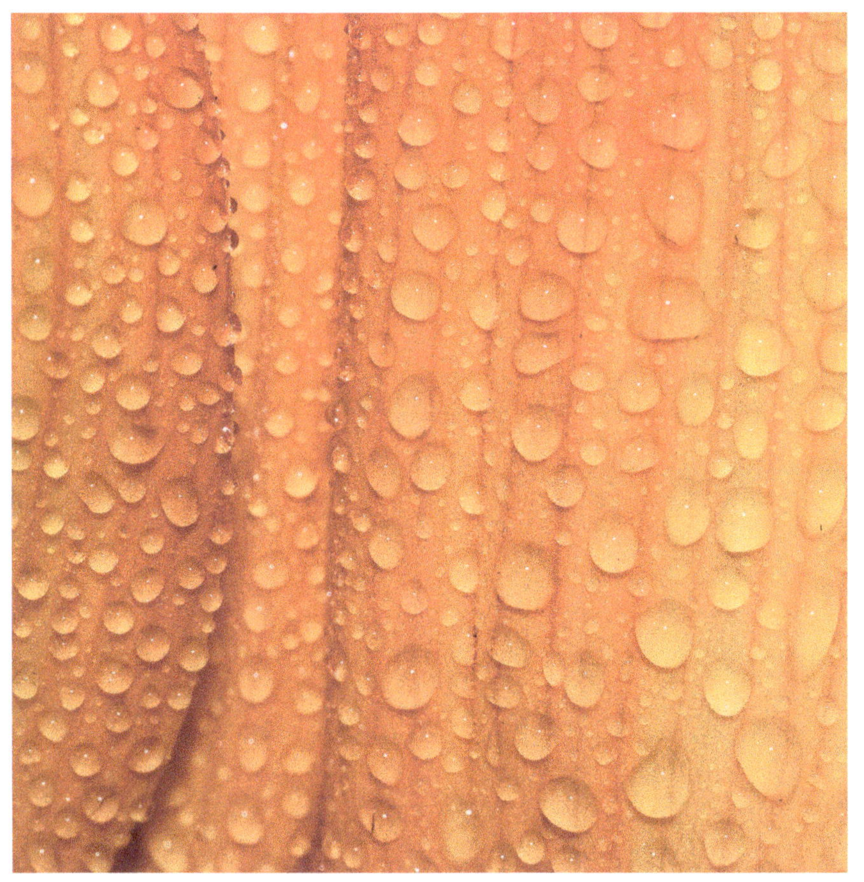

Dutch Orange, Saffron, Amber,

and Minium—an ultra-bright orange

for manuscript illustration

Artists, monks, and scientists explored them all—

Saffron, was the most expensive spice on earth,

not only the color for Buddhist robes,

but a bath salt for Cleopatra,

and a hopeful aphrodisiac for the rest of the world.

Paleontologists thrilled at insects occluded

in amber—searching for clues to DNA in vain.

Artists loved the fiery, intense shade of ginger—

Titian, Modigliani, especially Rossetti,

and his Brotherhood of Pre-Raphaelites.

Redheads, redheads, redheads, all the rage—

more artists jumped to the zing of orange,

like Munch, Gauguin and Van Gogh—

and the best comment of all is attributed

to Kandinsky, "Orange has confidence,

like a man convinced of his own power."

Oranja glad I told you?

ONE TOUCHED ME ON THE SHOULDER

She landed softly and fluttered twice,
I sensed I should not turn my head

After all, when you enter a butterfly garden,
shouldn't you be shy as a geisha?

Keep your head turned left and down,
float along the greenery,

carrying the white-winged one
with opaque dots on your shoulder

Near an open pineapple where ants crawl,
a second bewinged beauty alights

This one a marigold-orange,
framed with lace and black velvet fringe

Will Cabbage White and Painted Lady
nod to each other as I pass?

I think not, because as I pivot to the right,
whiteness grazes my neck

A fierce competitor, the Lady lifts aloft

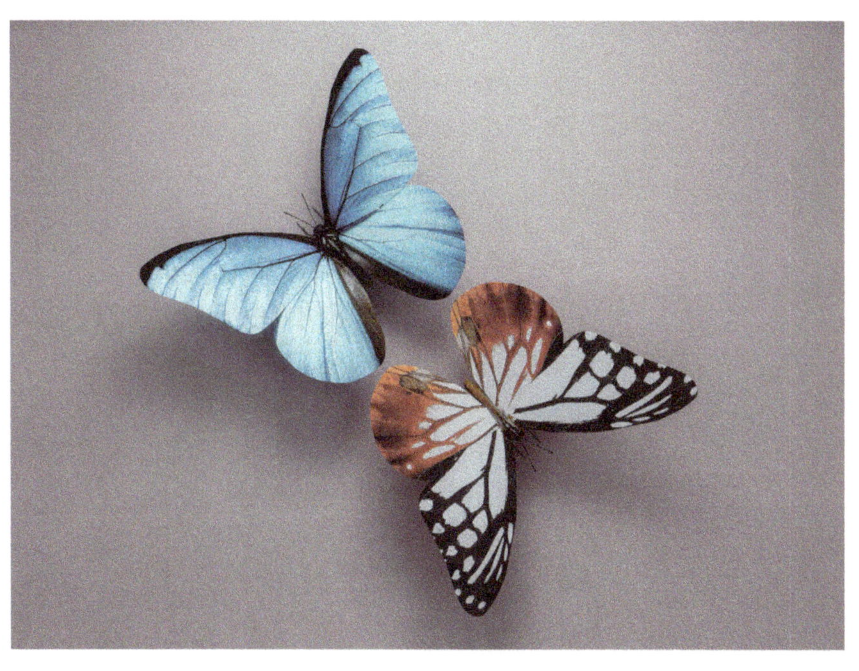

THE PRICE WE PAY FOR YELLOW

Ponder seldom heard-of kinds of yellow,
evoking symbols of mystery, good, and evil,
like peril, and poison, and power of pharaohs,
or smiley faces to send when we're gleeful.

Take *gold*, Klimt's portrait of Adele Block-Bauer,
made from slim gold sheets hammered from coins
glued to canvas. Similar to gold leaf woven into hair
of Botticelli's *Birth of Venus*, locks falling to loins.

Imperial yellow, pounded from foxglove roots
into paste, became dyes for gowns of royalty—
Silks worn in the Forbidden City by certain recluses,
like China's Qing Empress dowager in 1903.

Gamboge, from Cambodia in the 1600s
was solidified sap of Garcinia trees—
When crushed and mixed in oil, was favored
by Rembrandt to highlight the hands of Jesus.

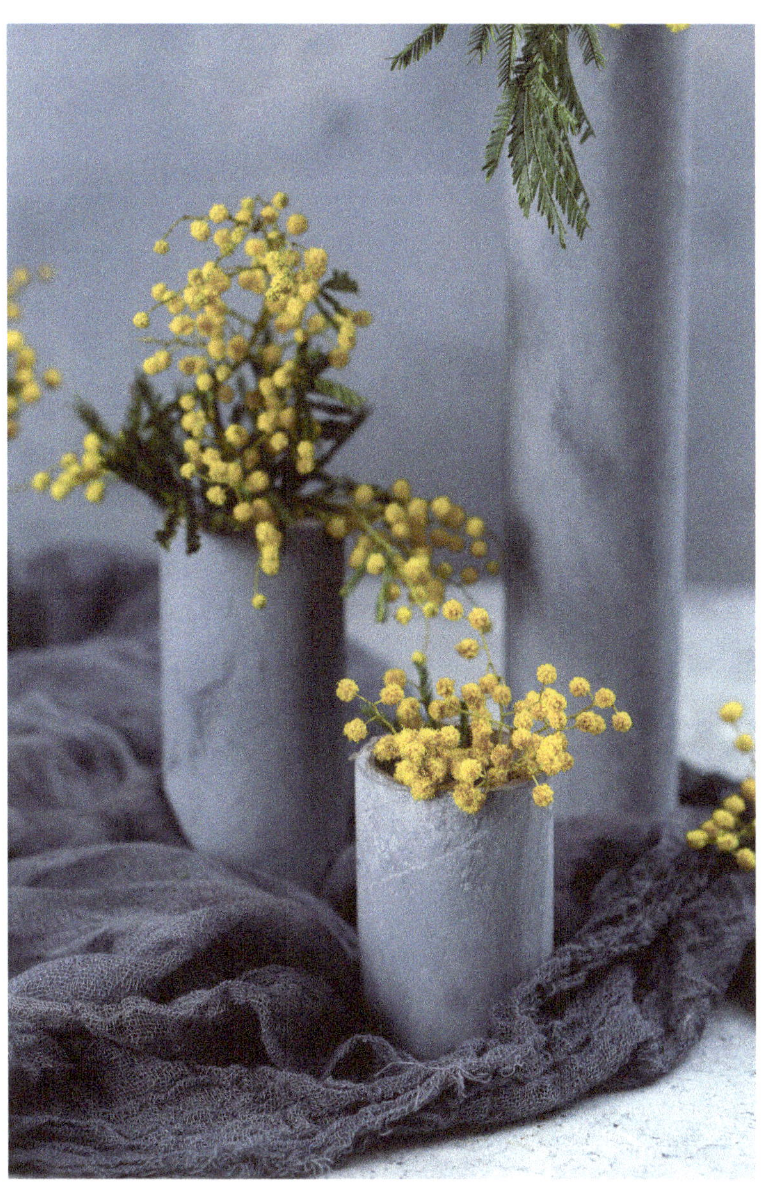

Besides *gamboge*, other yellows proved toxic—
Orpiment, mineral of arsenic sulfide, quite deadly,
its shining canary yellow illuminates the Book of Kells
and Taj Mahal walls, but reacts with lead poorly.

Van Gogh adored *chrome yellow*, from crocoite,
an unstable mineral. Sunflower after sunflower,
bright warm yellow popping from a vase in 1888,
but lead chrome darkened with age, like real-life bowers.

Lead-tin yellow, blonde, acid, chrome, and Naples,
more hues like Indian yellow—made from cow urine
Why the chase by artists to improve their materials?
An urgent search for a gleaming bright version,

despite the warning of contamination and danger—
they chose ox gallstones, the outpour of volcanic sulphur,
the high cost of metallics. Former painters dared wagers
that more generations are bound to surpass and discover.

They'll go beyond Pantones, paint chips, enamels,
find novel ways to concoct hues on computers,
layer on tints and tones with Photoshop,
offer yellow artworks as NFTs, a new lustrous lucre.

Yellow into Yellow

—Carl Jung associated the color yellow with
  the psychic function of intuition.

I'm several Pantone colors, though many hues confuse
and yellow has a checkered rep:

> bright and cheerful
> cowardly and deceitful

I have moments of pale yellow:

> Loosely knotted skeins of yarn
> Gemstones of yellow jasper
> Citrine chakra of the solar plexus

Also, I am darker, a warning to be careful:

> Diamond-shaped danger signs
> Boxes of poison
> Beam of the accusing flashlight

Dare come with me beyond caution to read the signs:

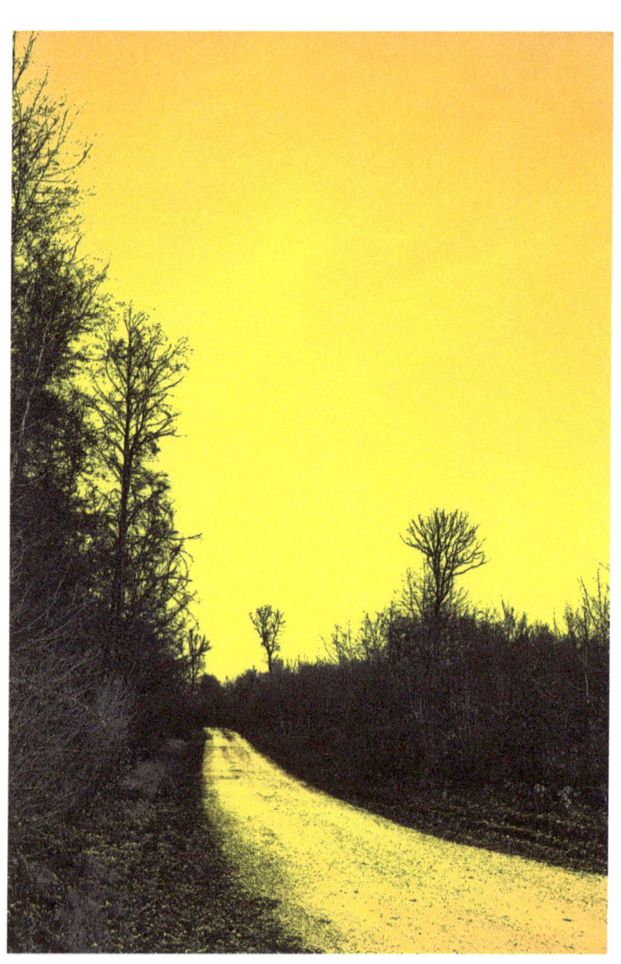

Don't cross the police tape
Don't slip and fall—Piso Mojado
Don't accelerate in the crosswalk

Dive in with me, you'll take daffodil risks:

> For, if I am fertile
> We could birth a fable
> Color of sunshine, we could bring joy

Yes, among Pantone colors, I'm hidden in full sight
Sometimes I arrive at places I don't know I'm going

If my wavelengths are the longest, do I have
magnetic power?

Yellow. I speak yellow:

> I can love my open passion
> I can be the clearest truth

CONTRADICTORY RED

Rocks were crushed, insects were bled,
   minerals and emulsifiers added,
      Scarlet, Crimson, Cherry, Madder
         Humans for decades rush to find Red

Artists keep reaching for Reds they made personal,
   push boundaries with gum, oil, and chemicals
      DaVinci and Rubens stained and emblazoned
         Rothko said Red was "fire and blood"

Red in the deep earth, comets, and stars,
   clay for geologists, Red Planet for Mars
      Astrologists explore universes widespread
         beyond black holes where blue stars appear Red

Red suggests ardent love, impassioned anger,
   stop signs and drama, martyrdom, power
      Symbol of fury, raging through psyches,
         lust and passion, fraught with danger

Red can seduce or portend good fortune,
   In China, people link crimson to luck and prosperity
      Red horns of the Devil can throw a strong hex
         Red light districts offer prostitutes and sex

Hues of Hematite, Pomegranate, Vermilion—
   Charlemagne, wore red leather shoes at his coronation
      Russia's flag turned Red for the Bolshevik Revolution
         Dragon's Blood, Burgundy, thinned with alizarin

Hence, a Red badge of courage, to raise a Red flag,
   to roll a Red carpet, or paint the town Red
      All tied up in Red tape, these stunning allusions
         only come to contradictory conclusions

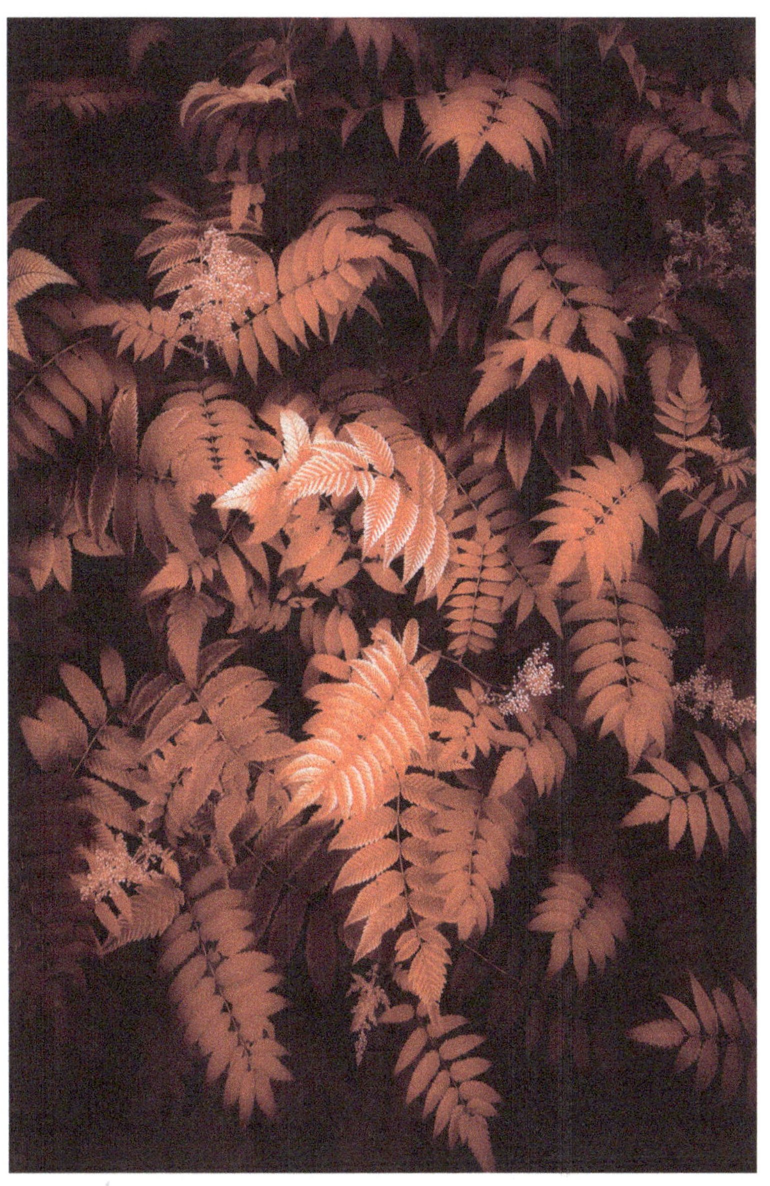

Three Sisters Ghazal

*—inspired by Robin Hall Kimmerer, author
of* Braiding Sweet Grass

Native Americans sow certain plants
     they know will survive together
Yellow corn, green beans, and
     pumpkin squash are raised together

Named Three Sisters since they resemble
     human family birth order
Corn, (eldest and wise), is planted first,
     preparing for their life together

Next sister, (undaunted), starts as a brown bean
     with a white bellybutton,
circles the stalks by wrapping her tendrils
     around so they can thrive together

When six inches high, Bean tells the third
     (the rebel) to elbow up into earth,
knowing squash leaves will provide nutrition,
     so sisters stay alive together

As youngest of three, with low-cupped leaves,
        Squash dances to her own tune,
The Three Sisters speak no words,
        but converse as they mature together

Sisters don't always prosper in families,
        birth differences make it hard at best
Nature brings lessons, turns envy to love,
        siblings strive through stress together

Each is able to survive on her own,
        but flourish when three harmonize
Golden corn, green pole beans, and
        rust squash deliver rich bounty together

RUBY NECKLACE

Sixty years ago, jeweler Nanda Lal Varma—
    Pedaled to our front door, Chanakyapuri, New Delhi
    Laid a black velvet cloth on the living room rug
    Spilled a bag of precious stones, started his sketch

Heart-shaped gold filigree tree, curlicues of branches and leaves—
    Decked with regal red birds, splashing crystal water
    A lacey breastplate studded with rubies, diamonds, pearls,
    the heirloom necklace my Mom left for me

I wore it to the Kennedy Center not long ago, rubies cascading—
    Down the deep décolletage of my green silk dress,
    Pearls spreading across frosted gold branches,
    Diamonds aglow, I was almost

Mom—
    Floating into Covent Garden for the opening of Swan Lake
    Toasting with champagne at the Ambassador's State dinner
    Waltzing with Iqbal Singh at the Delhi Golf Club Gala Ball

As the conductor swept up his baton for the finale of *Turandot*—
    Chandeliers sprayed showers of diamonds across the
        orchestra
    Red velvet chairs rose in perfect harmony above the
        Box Circle
    Guests twirled upward in corkscrew turns from the balcony

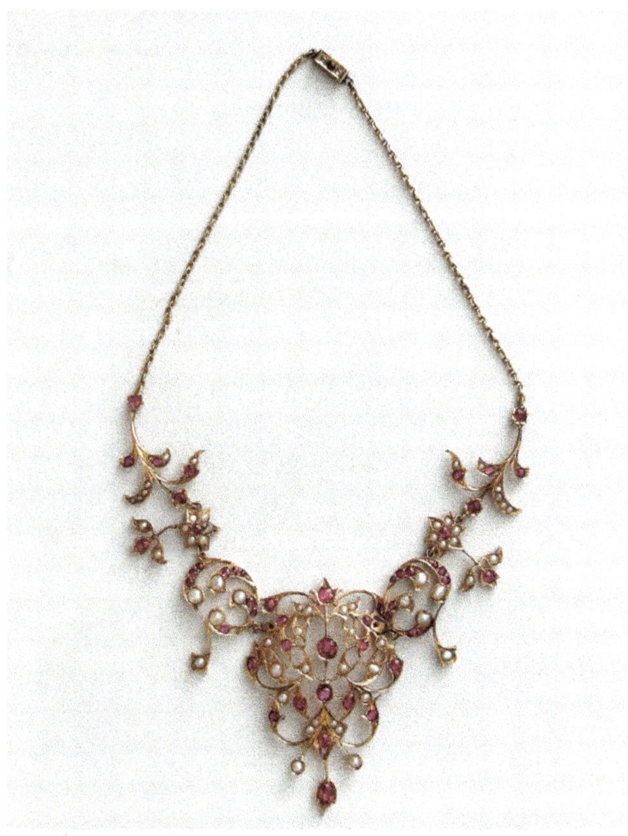

For a moment, the world was in unison, floating—
    Nanda Lal Varma cycled by, bike streamers riffling
    Scarlet birds sparkled, iridescent leaves shimmered
    I felt a gentle tap on my sternum as I lifted my arms

Mom's reminder to keep my shoulders back and head high—
    My first ballet teacher, she was exacting about port-de-bras
    First one to take me to the Opera too. Smiling, she bowed
    Playing to the gallery right through the skylight

QUADRUPLE RONDEL

—inspired by a visit to Stonehenge, a massive
stone circle erected in the late Neolithic period
in Wiltshire, England, about 2500 BCE

Stonehenge first appears as theater in the round
A ring of massive stones upright—
but horseshoes within circles within mounds
leave new visitors questioning their eyesight.

All the stones appear dark grey under clouds,
but sunshine reveals the original white—
Stonehenge first appears as theater in the round
A ring of massive stones upright.

Some called this sacred site a campground
to honor the dead, cremate at the site.
Others deemed it a healing place for pagans at night,
all knew it as a solar timepiece for the compound—
Stonehenge first appears as theater in the round.

Stonehenge for eons, mysterious and spiritual,
sounds of wonder and prayer hummed in unison.
Inner circle Bluestones were said to be musical,
stones "sang" when struck by those in communion.

Gathering together for comfort was ritual,
farmers could leave their fields only seldom—
Stonehenge for eons, mysterious and spiritual,
sounds of wonder and prayer hummed in unison.

Voyeurs have come to see the incredible—
a stadium of stones, where many truths are hidden.
Nothing known for sure, except the rule of sun,
the secrets of astronomy and religion contestable,
Stonehenge for eons, mysterious and spiritual.

Stonehenge was meant to be an unbroken circle
of two Sarsen stones linked by a third horizontal—
Like mortice and tenon, repeated on the external
ring, Bluestones in the center formed the internal.

Placed to line up with moments that were seasonal,
certain stones marked the exact time of solstices.
Stonehenge was meant to be an unbroken circle,
chains of Sarsen stones topped by horizontals.

Northeast "Heel Stone" threw light into the middle,
marking the height of summer. Sarsens
on the Southwest cast cold mid-winter darkness,
the last sunset that ended feasts and festivals.
Stonehenge was meant to be an unbroken circle.

Stonehenge, whether sundial or burial ground
hosts pillars of graffiti gray and lichen white—
Bodies below are hidden, antler bones are found,
all colors change under rain or in bright sunlight.

Among emerald English fields, beauty resounds,
Bluestones dragged from Wales, deep dolerite.
Stonehenge, whether sundial or burial ground,
hosts pillars of graffiti gray and lichen white.

Red stains on fallen stones abound,
where water turns iron to shades of hematite—
People divine stories that may not be right,
curious viewers will be forever spellbound,
Stonehenge, mystically sundial and burial ground.

THE WAY KIDS SEE IT

My favorite color is ahhhnge,
explains Joseph at his pre-school easel

And mine is lellow
cause it makes me sunny, responds Emily

Poppy, sporting pink ribbons, boasts
I have three Barbies

Molly, in black tee-shirt with skulls,
replies, *You are an ass-toe*

Matthew announces that he likes baloo,
and pours it all over the floor

Miss Angela in her turquoise apron,
covered with fingerpaints, smiles

and cheers on students who choose
porple, gween, even *dork gray*

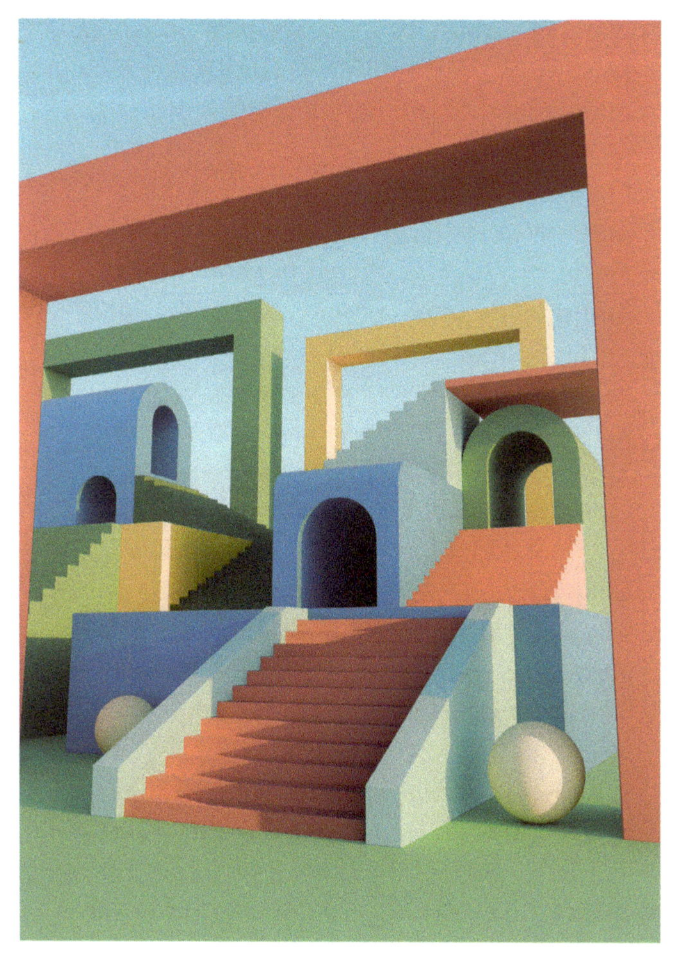

A Case of the Stripes

Long ago, stripes were a symbol of shame
worn by criminals, outcasts, and hangmen
In spite of that, rainbows, candy canes, flags,
and sailors' blue-and-whites saved them

Gone were the dark stripes of prisoners
and low-cast "Devil Cloth" of prostitutes
European royals coveted purple stripes
and remade them a high-fashion attribute

Colorful stripes, no longer low-cast,
are considered bold, daring, and vibrant
Designers make them a fashion attribute,
choosing coquelicot, peach, and amaranth

Stripes are bold, daring, and vibrant,
like goldenrod, zaffre, and annato
Embraced and renamed by designers—
think Armani, Chanel, and Siriano

Whether tones of yellow, blue or orange,
artists through time repeat bands of lines
Think Paul Klee, Rothko, and Hepworth,
Barnett Newman, Gene Davis, and Kline

Artists through time repeat bands of lines—
Bridget Riley, Gerhard Richter, Dan Flavin
Regarded as masters of modern abstraction,
distinguished in oil paint, textiles, and neon

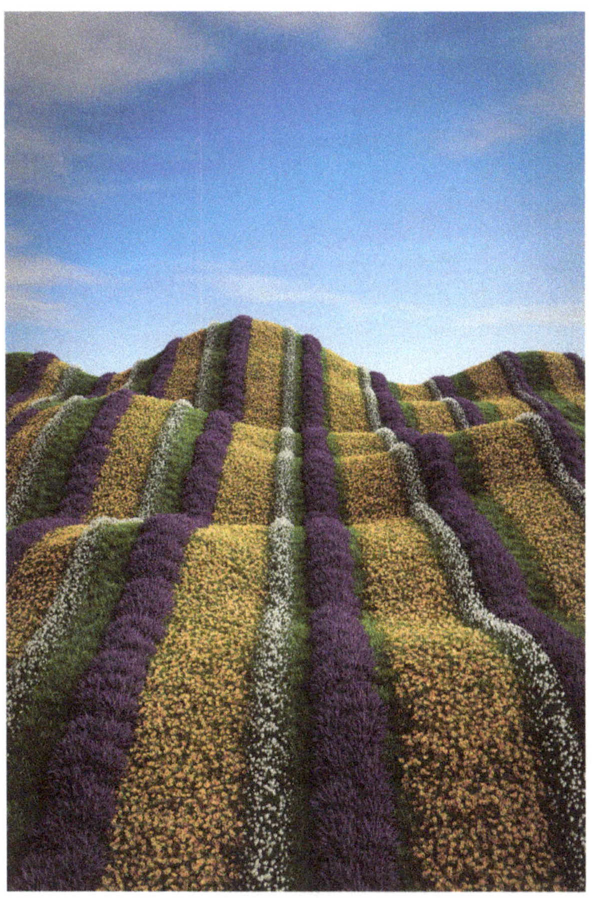

Artists through time are inspired by music—
Linling Lu's *Soundwaves*' striped wheels,
Handel's *Messiah* with memorable lyrics,
like "and with His stripes we are healed"

A final homage to sheer beauty of stripes
comes in business, not nature or fashion
To "Earn Your Stripes" is to gain respect
and acceptance in profession, raw passion

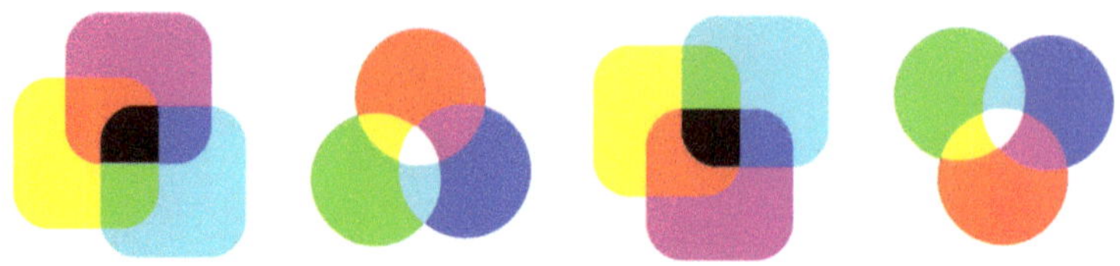

PMS AND CMYK, RGB AND HEX

I hate acronyms— can't tell if they
stand for a disease, COPD, a political group,
PAC, or a prescription, RX.

But I love my PMS. No, not *that* one—
It's my PMS Pantone Marketing System
box of print colors, all 1755 of them.

I don't take my orange slacks
and brown jacket along to shop, I bring
orange Pantone color cards to find

a yummy sweater or this season's blouse
Pumpkin and *sage? Cantaloupe*
and *mushroom?*

Oh, hooray—a standard system for
describing colors. But wait—fashionistas
and car companies make up their own!

White becomes pearl or glacial,
brown turns to *coffee bean, fawn,*
or *Texas tea,* even *root beer.*

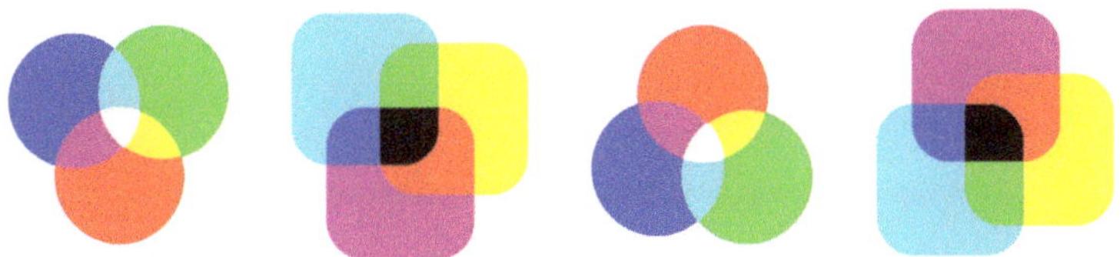

Oh, good lord, my printer
*takes CMYK ink—Cyan, Magenta,
Yellow, Black.*

No, the clever inkjet printer
sprays out tiny pixel dots in batches
to produce various shades and tints—

a sprinkle of choices—my business logo
*could be jade, capri, or sea foam green,
cornflower, turquoise, or sapphire.*

Years back, when I turned
from art to the screen, I learned
that online colors differed from print.

All that I knew about primary colors,
pure red, yellow, blue, RYB, had
changed for television—

At first, I thought my production
mentors were just plain dumb when
they talked about the standard, RGB.

Oh jeez, RGB is the opposite
of CMYK. Mix all RGBs,
and you get white.

Remove all RGBs, you get black—
It's all about electronic illumination
of pixels on your screen.

HEX, a shorthand for RGB, assigns
different numbers: *Tomato*, an orange,
is HEX FF6347; RGB 255,99.

Oh my, so confusing, irritating!
My color TV is called LG, but
that's another story—

Originally, it meant "Lucky Goldstar"
in South Korea for a TV brand—
gold, the lucky color for sales.

In the USA, LG is promoted
as "Life's Good." Electronics
and colors can turn you on your head.

My band width is on overload,
my hard drive too full—
that's why I hate ACRNMS.

POOR BROWN

Mummy is a color—made from bitumen, ground bones
    of Egyptians, three thousand years old
In 1904, apothecaries sold the rich brown powder
    to staunch blood and treat epilepsy
Mummy can also be pale, like leftover remains
    of mammal bodies
No wonder I can't eat brains or tripe

Sepia, equally gross, is ink and mucus
    squirted from octopi, squid, and cuttlefish
But Leonardo da Vinci found it to be
    a gorgeous shade for his sketches
Ultimately, in the context of photography,
    it depicted romance and nostalgia
I still can't bear the offal of cuttlefish

Russet, a more precise color, also changed
    in symbolism over time
Once a rough wool cloth, worn by cowherds,
    ploughmen and corn threshers,
it transformed into a sign of honesty, humility
    and manliness
I do enjoy reddish-brown potatoes

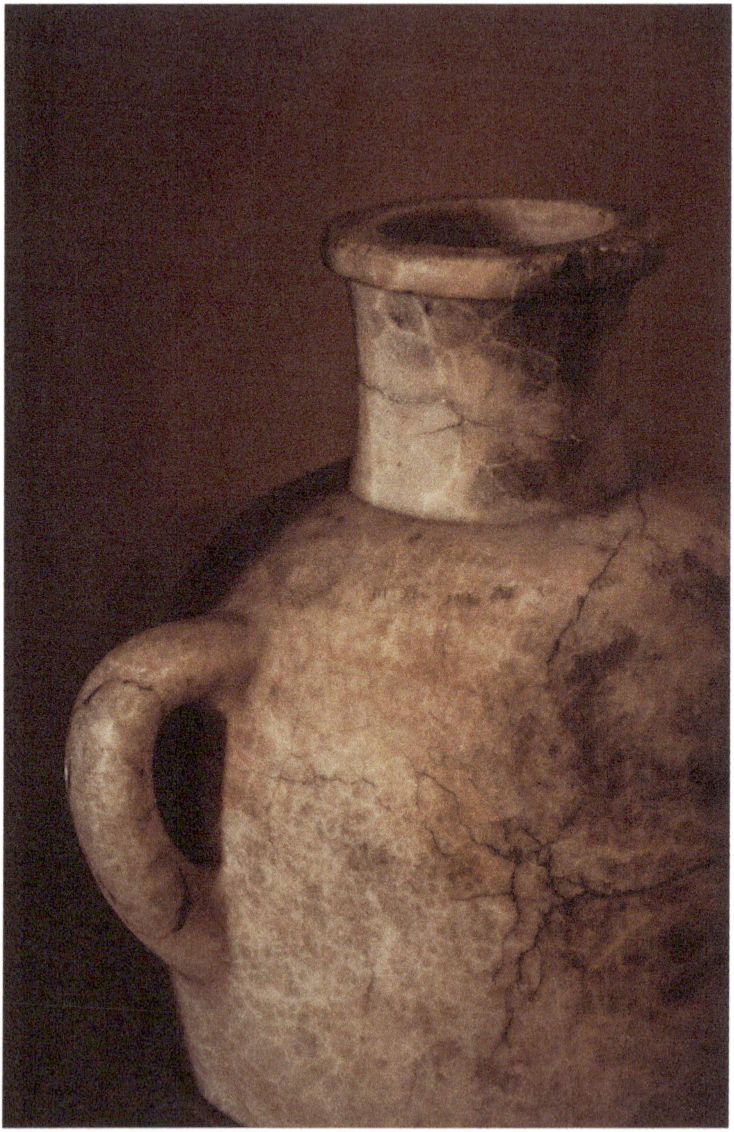

Speaking of manliness, Buff is slang
        for "Buffalo," the buttery color
of tanned ox leather. Buff is not for naked,
        but a popular shade of soldiers' garb—
George Washington chose buff for his army,
        eventually popular for gentlemen's overcoats
I eat neither buffalo burgers, nor smooth suede chamois

Moreover, it will not be a surprise that
        another brown, Khaki,
is an Urdu word for "dusty," useful camouflage
        for military uniforms in Pakistan
Cheap white cotton—soaked in mud, tea,
        coffee or curry powder
Hmmmm. Like Indian food?

It's hard to show gratitude for brown,
        although it is an attractive color to me
And, artists like Correggio and Rembrandt loved
        the paint it made for deep shadows
Still, khaki comes from earth pigments—iron oxides,
        ochers—a dense brown, like liver
In summary, when we think of brown, the color
        of mud, filth, and shi* come to mind

I don't need to tell you what else I don't eat

Rebirth on the Metro Quay

I have gone and come back to life
two times in full color

Here's how—

Knife sliced my thumb,
viscous red

Tetanus shot, pure gunpowder,
blinding black. I faint once more

Now this—

Metro roars, train windows slant,
stations slip by, light dims
Cold sweat pours down my chest

So frightening to fade, go
feeble, as rising black-out
mounts my breastbone

And then it's done—

A woman sees me slump,
yanks me toward the door,
lays me down

Gray cement bench is cool
What I took to be disappearing
comes back clear

Neon-aproned station master
leaning over me,
"Did you eat breakfast?"

Back at work, I drink
mango juice, eat a banana,
remove my multicolored scarf

Relief—indigo, amethyst, cyan
seep pigment anew

At Last

Ice blue wind rubs the trunks and shivers stick branches,

a shroud of dull clouds dare away color

Bumblebees wonder if spring will ever answer

Bats worry the snow will refuse to abandon,

Mean sleet and dirty hail cause skunks to shudder

Ice blue wind attacks trunks and breaks stick branches

Wood frogs won't leap, frigid air makes them anxious,

snakes furrow further in deep holes, cursing another

cold spell. Exhausted bees plead spring to answer

Hark! Rumor has it that warm sunlight might chance it

Hedgehogs lumber forward to shake off their torpor,

golden breezes caress trunks, cheer buds on the branches

Forsythia appears like fuzzy beards on fat bushes

Bulbs push up tulips that flame in tricolor

Bees buzz around cherry trees searching pink chances

Magenta azaleas peek down at shamrock grasses,

box turtles emerge seeking warmth to recover

Only soft winds pass the trunks and wave branches,

Bumblebees smile with dizziness . . . spring advances

THE LIGHT IS DIFFERENT, COLORS FEEL IT

Deep red hibiscus plants still flower in flocks

along the sidewalks, they grow tall—4 to 10 feet.

One bloom, poppy-bright, is as big as a dinner plate,

paper-thin, it will only last one to three days,

but you'd never guess that with its resolute redness.

Strong color rises as flames within other flowers too—

Canna lilies, late-summer bloomers,

grow fiery reddish-orange "flags" that shoot up

from shiny dark-green foliage.

As temperatures slyly drop,

other early bloomers turn in their hues, close down,

circle their stalks, bend to the dry earth.

Oversized sunflower heads,

dangle heavily in brown apology,

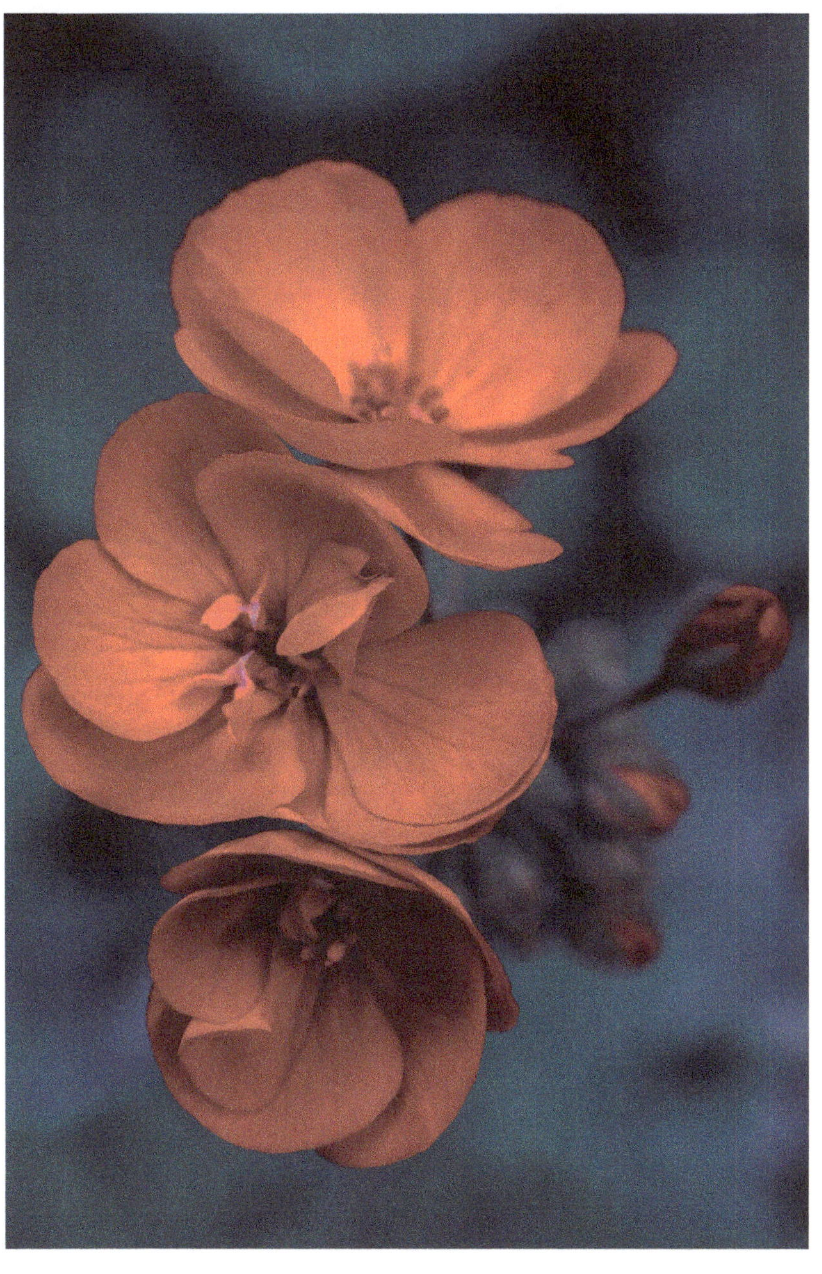

pleading with their curving stalks to hang on a bit longer.

Frantic birds—house finches and sparrows—

flutter, like frenetic hummingbirds,

to suck out dried seeds from downward-facing discs.

Earlier, with upright faces in proud-yellow extremis,

they stretched high and sturdy during their run in the sun.

Squirrels, even the albino one,

who has little chance of camouflage at any time of year,

scampers about nut-collecting,

nibbling every other one to fatten up for the fury of fall.

Everyone knows—

the hibiscus, the sunflower, the squirrel who can't hide easily

Everyone knows—

the crickets and cicadas trilling out their mournful blues,

Everyone knows—

summer is bowing out.

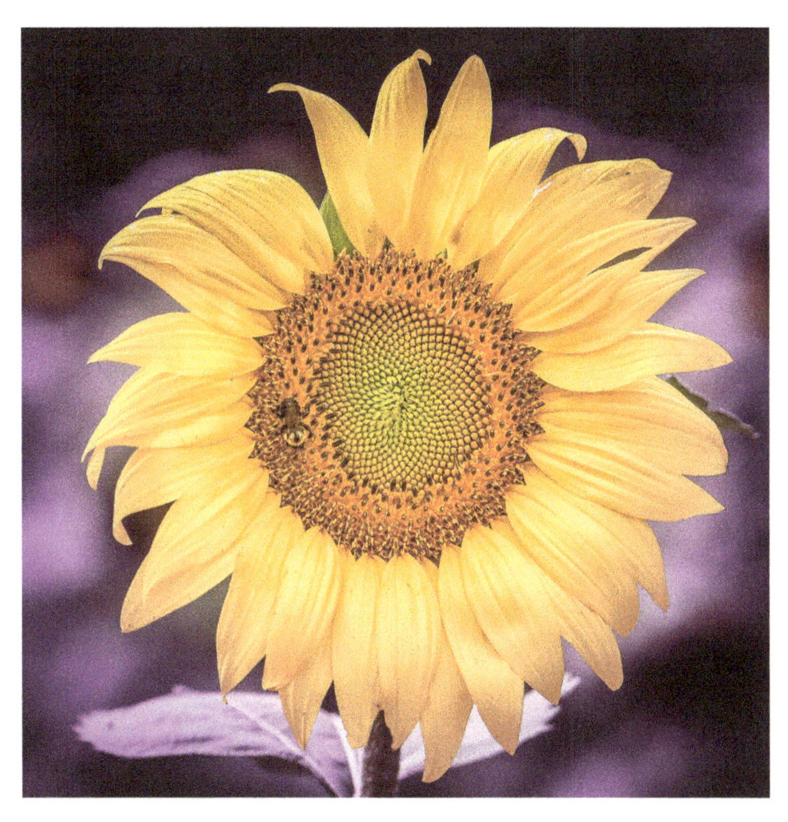

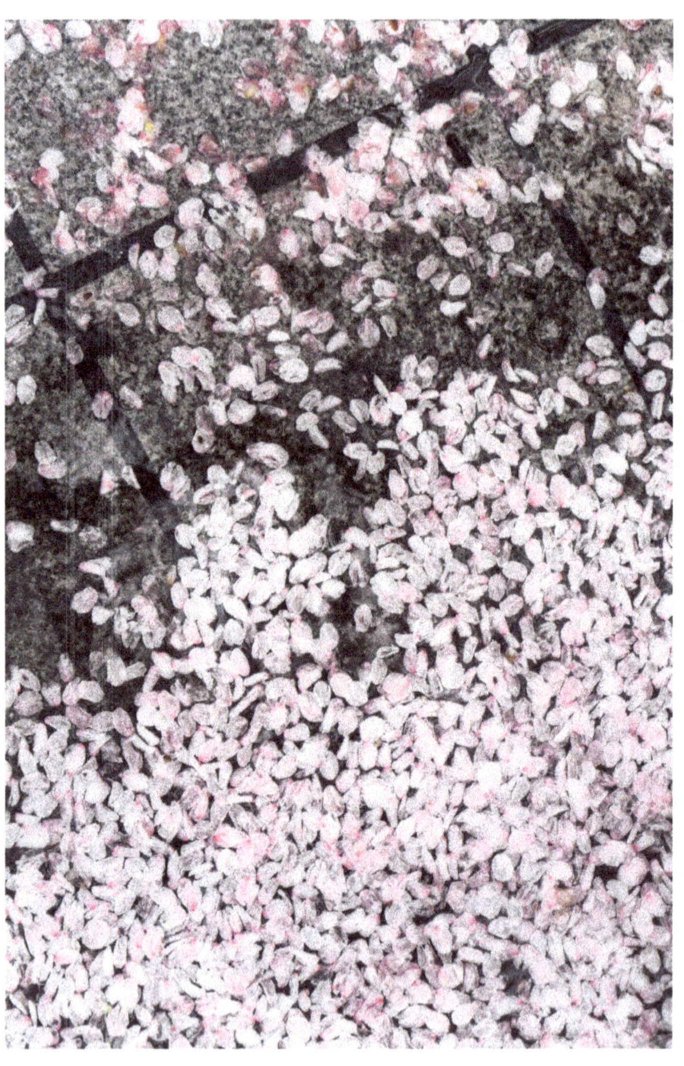

Farewell to Glorious Pink at the Basin

—inspired by Gerard Manley Hopkins

Praise the blossoms of spring with "Hosanna!"
Westerly, breezily, wafting, and sensuous
Sing to all the unknown and most glorious!
Yesterday, cherry trees fluttered me on
Today, all dampened, a slant rain fell down
A million delicate confettis loosen
pinkish-gray lace on the carpeting, brown
Onlookers, who once paraded, are gone

But all for this! A duck glides by—
emerald, shimmering, confident trail
Trees watch, they neither mourn, nor sigh
Seasons do rise, some withered oak will fail
But orange tulips push into the sky—
Chorus of ripples and branches chant "Hail!"

Two Crickets, Two Bees, and a Hydrangea

Last morning two brittle black crickets

lay upside down inside the doorway,

last night the mourning dove slowed its moan.

Last swim at dusk — shadows rippled

over the purple mountain,

a single car rumbled across gravel.

Two early trees turn red in the meadow,

two huge yellow bees hover in and out,

but don't find what they need.

The hydrangea bush, so stalwart all summer,

its shriveling blossoms wrestle to stay white.

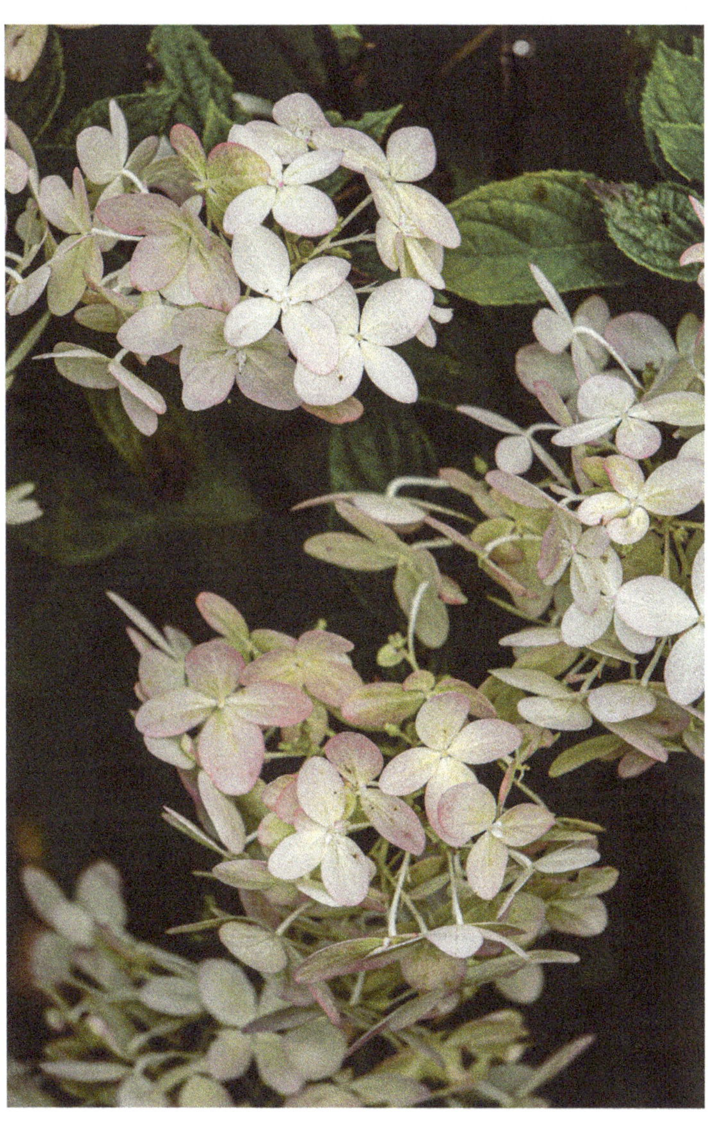

STONE BRIDGE

—Marjorie Merriweather Post bought
   Hillwood Estate in Washington, D. C.
   in 1955 and soon decided that her
   home would be a museum that would
   inspire and educate the public. The
   stone bridge is in the Japanese Garden.

I walk the long flat
stone atop the stream,
before I sit
Cascading waterfalls
descend close by,
trying to quiet me

Less distracted now,
listening more,
I turn from showy
magenta azaleas
to examine
that dull flat stone

Lying resolutely serene,
as eternities of water
flow under, the stone
knows it is a bridge,
and guards
what dwells below

Silent, cool,
resting prostrate,
the gray stone recognizes
baby granite pebbles
peering upward. Its voice

rumbles to the underside
It has tales to tell,
absorbing life
for centuries, and
wants to preserve
precious family history

Baby stone bodies below,
with the same amber
and teal markings
that have faded on
the dark slate bridge above,
are waiting for their story

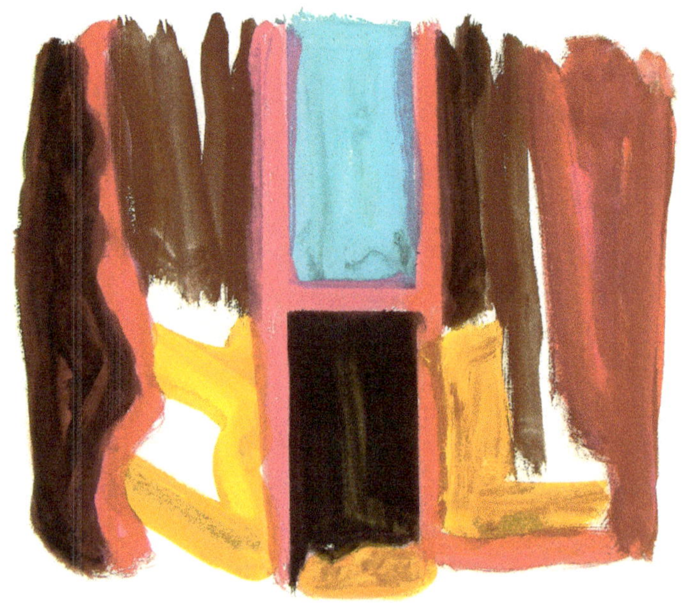

SHADES OF ANGER

—after reading about color theory by
Johann Wolfgang von Goethe and Joseph Albers

Broad brushstrokes of rage are red,
streaked by dark brown doomsday dread.
But, mine hold peaks of bluish darts,
emerging from black where hatred starts.

TINTS OF ANGUISH

—after reading about color theory by
Johann Wolfgang von Goethe and Joseph Albers

My paintbrush turns tan into blurred arcs of soot,
underscores grief that knots in my gut.
Braided shapes tighten to clot in the center,
burnt brown loneliness groans in surrender.

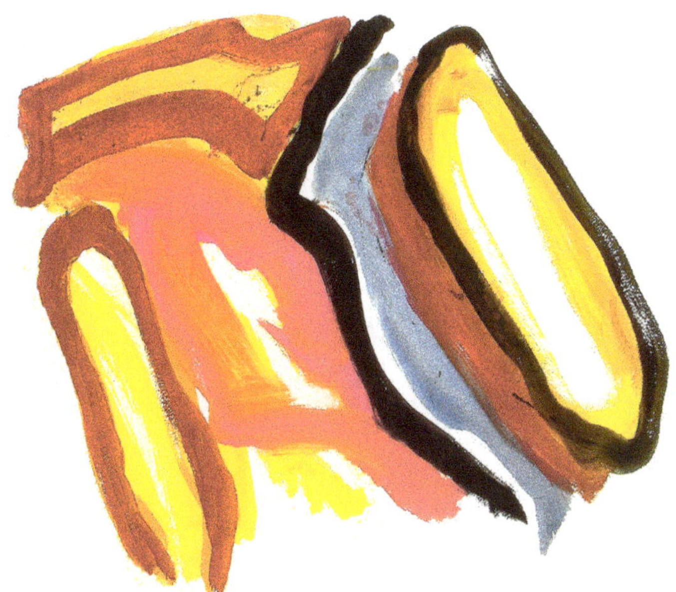

THE BOOK OF PASSWORDS

—after Al Zolynas's "Considering the Accordion"

The idea of it is unappealing at best. The pages, like
a dictionary of my life—some dog-eared by overuse,
some empty. Nothing on the "Q" page. Dingy off-
white cover, encircled by a worn-out black elastic band.
Stowed away in far reaches of my stained desk, two old
password books lie fallow. The mottled black and white
notebook is the elder, the stiff cardboard conference
gift, the newer, but still outdated. Opening them, I am
an intruder, pretending I remember what the URLs *are*,
that appear to be forgotten grocery lists—Hungryroot,
Shatila, Rodman's, Snapfish, Ugly Mug.

Evn my current one is packed with cross-outs, do-overs,
a yellow sticky note from the early pandemic, with
the address of NYU Langone Hospital in case I had a
deadly emergency while visiting NYC. But for all that, I
cling to this tiny Bible, its fading cover still soft leather,
the inner tan liner still smooth felt, the pages still there,
but limp. For a moment, it is divine—a prayer book
when my credit cards are stolen, twenty-six psalms in
order from Apple to Zoom, my passport in uncertain
times, a moment of silence for all that remains.

JOY

Seeing dolphins in duos on the horizon
swimming like sailboats, rocking side to side

Dancing triplets across the grass and
playing "Hallelujah" by Leonard Cohen

The crunch of fennel atop fresh greens
Sounds and smells of rich coffee beans
perking

A perfect dollop of cream in the cup
Red wine and ultra-dark chocolate

The softest lemon cotton tee shirt
Trousers grazing hips and flowing

Wrist warmers with fingers sticking out
Darn-Tough socks and German ankle boots

Saying each consonant, followed by a,e,i,o,u
Ta, tee, tie, toe, two!

Wa, wee, why, whoa, wuu!
Color shoots out in sparks

SERENITY HUES

I thought I knew what serenity was without color—

   a meditation of repeating murmurs,

      low chants from the monastery on the hill,

         muffled Tibetan bells traveling the valley

But then I see the sap green lily pad, pushing

      from under a wash of umber muck and gray stems,

         surrounded by endless ripples of dusky ultramarine

Fragile lotus flower

      bursts forth, its seedpod heart of cadmium yellow tickled by

         stringy strands of peach, wriggling bean sprouts

A crown ringed by petals, reaching up like candlelight flames,

      pale pools of lavender, thin stripes of whisper white

         tipped in violet

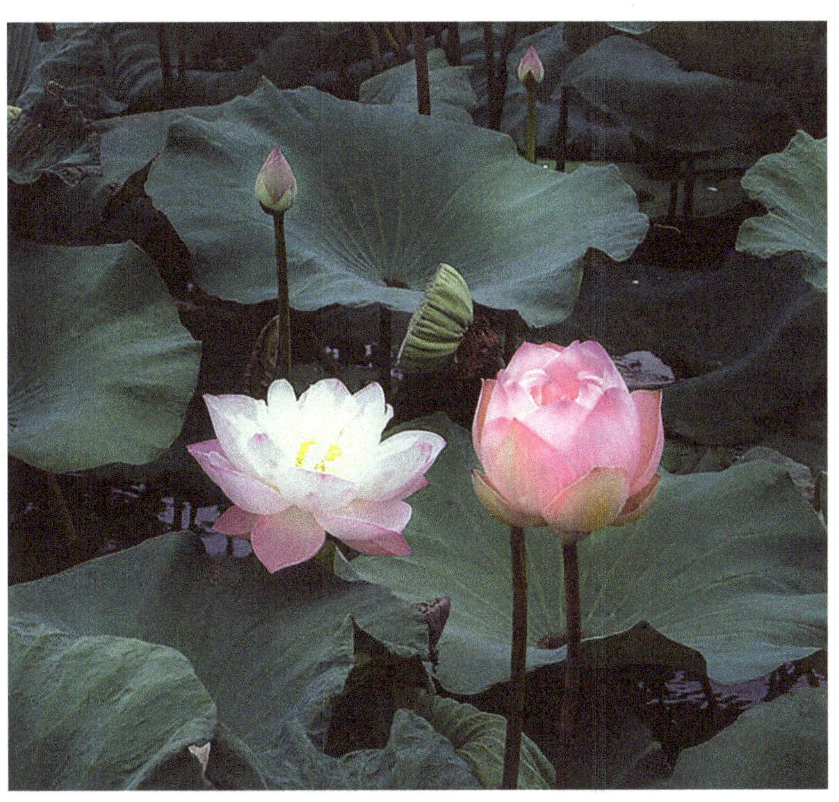

M-A-C-K

"When I walk half as fast, I notice twice as much"
—Tara Brach, meditation expert

And it is true . . .

Walking slowly down 43rd St. toward Madison,
a scene strikes me—green wooden box platform,
a self-contained bleacher stand with three steps,
three caramel leather chairs, steel armrests,
a scatter of shoe brushes, boot polish tins,
and several flannel buffing cloths.

A gaggle of foot-traffic New Yorkers pass by,
focused, fast-moving, headed to work. At first,
I go by . . . but take the time to reconsider, turn,
go back to the stand, and ask the man waiting there,
"Can you shine these?"

My old black leather boots are dull.
I climb the steps and introduce myself.
He says Good to meet you, Lee.
I'm M-A-C-K, like the truck. Where are you from?
I say, "Washington DC,"
he says, *Oh, the MAD city!"*

We laugh, and I ask if I can take his picture.
Take a picture of your boots, he suggests,
A "Before" and "After" when I'm done.
He's shaped like a truck—broad chest, sturdy
legs, wide smile. Black pants, green apron,
black sweatshirt over blue tee shirt, cap.
I ask how long he's been there. *Sixteen years,*
same place since the first day I set up.

People stride by and greet him, and he them.
One guy drops a plastic baggie on the step
below my chair.

Mack rolls my trousers up my ankles,
cleans the boots with red vinegar, rubs in
black polish from a can, coats the rim
with an unknown shiny black liquid,
and goes to town—brushing. And brushing.
Buffing, and rebuffing, especially the toes.

He charges $8.00, and takes a picture
with my camera—first of my *"After"* boots,
and then of me on the chair, my wooly gray hat
pulled low, grin wider than ever.
As I get down and follow the morning walkers,
he waves, *Bye, Lee, take care in the MAD city.*

I don't know the name of the guy
who left the baggie, or the next guy
with scuffed brown shoes ready for a shine.
But I do have a picture of it all:
the bench, the chairs, the steps,
the plastic baggie with two sandwiches,
(pale white bread with single
dark orange slices of baloney).

And M-A-C-K, like the truck.

KING TUT AND I HAVE A TUNA SANDWICH

—when I saw gold, gold, and more gold,
  with flashes of coral, royal blue and turquoise...

I explore The Golden King: The World of Tutankhamun
exhibition at the National Geographic, and I buy the catalog.
Then, in line at the café, I order a six-inch flatbread with tuna,
pepper-jack cheese, olives, and dill pickles and begin to read. I
turn to the page with the funerary mask of the 19-year-old King
Tut. A gold cobra and vulture, studded in turquoise, adorn his
forehead. His black eyes stare up at me as I bite into tuna fish,
crunch a rippled Sun chip, and swallow a swig of root beer. I
study the Golden King—how he died, how he was elevated
from King to God by weighing his heart balanced against the
Feather of Truth. The Egyptians had to follow all the steps
of mummification so the Pharoah would have everything he
needed in the afterlife: insert a hook in the nose and pull out the
brain; remove all internal organs and let them dry; place lungs,
intestines, stomach and liver in alabaster canopic jars; place the
heart back in the body; rinse the inside of the body with plum
wine; cover the corpse with salt (natron) for 70 days; stuff the
body with linen to retain its shape; wrap the body from head to
toe in linen cloth bandages; place body in a box (sarcophagus).

The Egyptians believed the soul left the body at death, and
that for eternal life, the body and soul had to be reunited. To
survive in the afterlife, the body would need food and water.
I'm still eating my lunch when I read that a key ritual and
last step before the burial was The Opening of the Mouth. A
special attendant would open the mouth of the mummy, using
an instrument made of gray stone, with a serpentine silver blade
shaped like the tail of a fish. Once he became a God, judged by
Osiris (God of the Afterlife), the Pharoah could breathe,

speak, and enjoy his treasures. There, in his glory, he would eat tasty treats, drink fine red wines, and listen to the cherished music of trumpets. Mouth open, he tasted roasted gazelle, any fish he desired, and whole wheat honey cakes. In concert with his music, I finish my last bite of tuna on whole wheat flat bread—and a chocolate chip cookie.

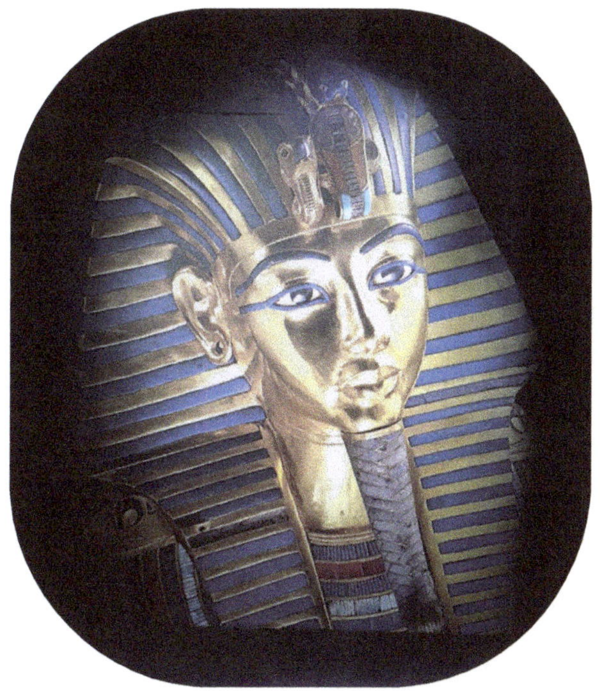

Note: Baudelaire wrote prose poems to rebel against classical versification. He dreamed of "a poetic prose, musical without rhyme or rhythm, supple and jerky enough to adapt to the lyric movements of the soul, to the undulations of reverie, to the somersaults of conscience."

—from Edward Hirsch's *A Poet's Glossary*

RECOMPOSE

I want to be dirt when I die—
not that I don't like cemeteries. I do.
But only because of the stories, not the bodies,
I want to be dirt when I die.

At the funeral home, they ask my friend
to identify her mother's embalmed colorless corpse.
No, I spurn the mahogany coffin, steel-lined,
to be lowered into a grave, encased by concrete.

I want to be dirt when I die—
no chemical perfumes, no open casket,
no taking up land that could be a playground,
a bird sanctuary, an orange grove.

I want to be covered with alfalfa and sawdust,
with tawny straw as a bed beneath my bones.
We'll dissolve together into bark-like pieces
to form an earthy floor, like pine needle mulch.

After all, the residue from the composting
will be given to families to throw over oceans,
where sediment may add silt to shore—
or to place under a peony bush like my mother's.

I want to be in the prayer hall of reconstitution,
not on an undertaker's table, nor burned to ashes—
because the price is too high,
because land and water are thirsting.

Let forest restoration folk spread me gently,
especially under willows and weeping firs.
Let me sink into the congregation of worms
and mushrooms; we'll send psalms aloft.

I want to be dirt when I die—
not that I don't like rituals. I do.
Bodies and bones become earth of the fields,
an epic higher than sky.

WHAT I SUSPECT ABOUT THE ARTIST AND THE GIRL

—a villanelle inspired by Vermeer's Girl in a Red Hat, 1669

He turns an oak panel upside down as an experiment
Covers up an old painting, a new subject appears
A sensuous girl created by him with deep sentiment

Her dashing vermillion beret, jaunty and elegant
Draws us in to his obsession about her
Generous brushy strokes, his new experiment

Wild dashes of light near dark, a distinct element
Liquid glaze on her eyes and lips sexually clear
A flush of pink on her cheeks reeks of deep sentiment

Perhaps the passion is part of *her* temperament
She turns to look, open-mouthed, implies certain fervor
Lush blue coat, red tipped hat, *his* crafty experiment

Slight tilt of head, flash of earrings suggest merriment
A bed in the background with slippers so near
Her come-hither posture hints mutual sentiments

A sharp cast of light from the right, shows his intent,
picture and story converge here
Quick abstractions of shape are his experiment
But love-filled realism proves his true sentiment

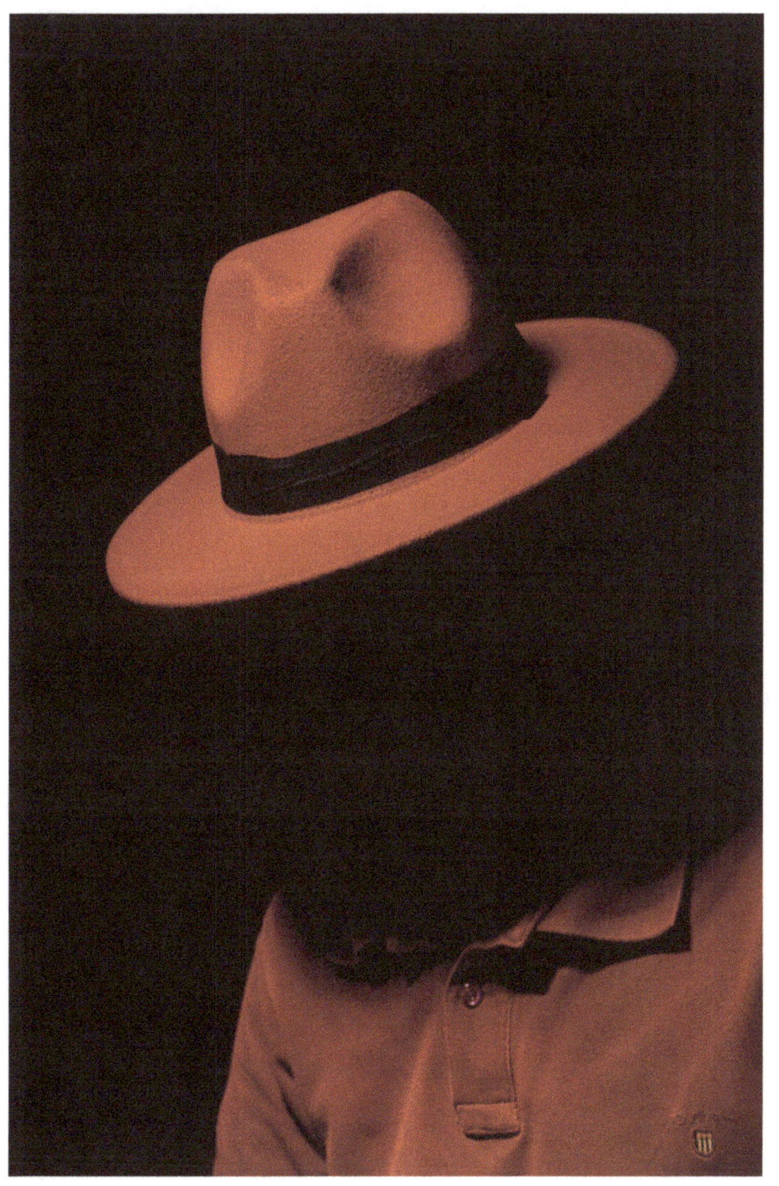

ABSTRACT SPLASH OR LITERAL WAR?

—inspired by Wassily Kandinsky's Improvisation 31, (Sea Battle), 1913

I see turbulence in roiling colors
He sees terrible struggle ahead
I sense angry reds moving in to crush the middle
He hears blasts of cannons rocking ships

I detect slender black masts,
tossed left and right, bluish-white ruffled sails
He sets the scene by explosions— orange and green,
diluted pools of sickly blood—yellow-orange

I focus on wild confusion framed by
a tieback curtain—a wash of yellow, a slash of gold
He insists on improvision and abstraction, yet
draws green hands, white fingers screeching

We agree that the middle mountain triangle
of white serves up a stage for dobs of deep blue,
restless marks of inky black, a stroke of malachite—
snakelike. He calls upon fervent color to electrify,

like a warning wire, he cautions about oncoming war
I cherish his conviction that humanity can
be transported by Art—blue imagination, red ovation,
the magenta of transformation. It peeks through

the heart of his canvas, offering the drawing pencil
with which he scribbles his signature. Despite the
ebony crow below, I marvel at the patches
of green he splashes for new faith, a cry for freedom

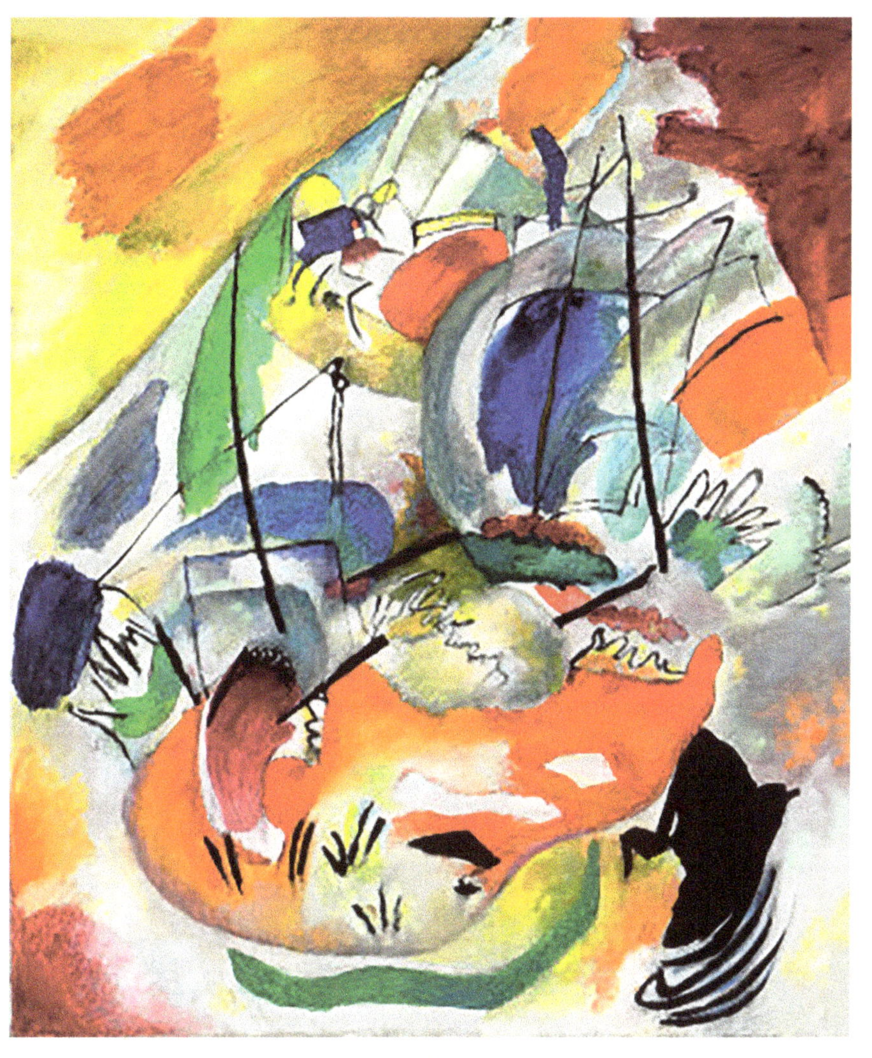

Portrait of an Artist, an Anguished Man

—after David Hockney's Portrait of an Artist (Pool with Two Figures), 1972

Waking early today, I head to the infinity pool on the deck—

Sunlight reflects on the rippling water, cerulean on top, turquoise

with wavy white lines on the vermiculite and cement flooring.

You may not know it, but I saw you come out fully dressed

in your mint-colored trousers and pink blazer,

picking up the glint of nearby crab-apple blossoms.

Beyond the pool is paradise,

five ranges of St. Tropez mountains,

darker green in the near, fading to mist in the far.

Two poplar trees stand side by side in the forest green setting,

once iconic of our union, now like Greek columns of the past—

Beauty and Grace, we once resembled those perfectly
    aligned trees,

now you remain single, resolute, staring down

as my body writhes. Movement of the water wobbles my limbs,

my body is mere flotsam, legs akimbo,

brain clouded in cobwebs. My head underwater as I
    breaststroke

toward you, you stand stark-still at the end of the pool,

looking down at my back, your hair in a blond feathered
    shag,

your tan leather loafers pointing me in the opposite
    direction.

Once my muse, you stare emotionless at my bareness,

while I shed tears underwater—

I know I must do a flip-turn when I reach you and cast away,

towards the spillover of infinity, falling to concrete below.

UNDERWATER

A woman with long chestnut hair sits

at the edge of the lake, crying,

combing.

Water absorbs her prayers, transports her sadness,

she slips in—

only the water knows this is not a baptism,

something far beyond that—

She's no mermaid, nor nymph, yet

when she swims, she glides, surrounded by spirits.

She lifts her black eyelashes,

water flows to the cavern of her soul.

Vodyanoy wrap their legs around her, a warm embrace,

she sheds her cream camisole. Using no airpipe,

she can breathe air or water easily,

velvety sea-pearl sand grazes her soles

when she chooses to land for a moment.

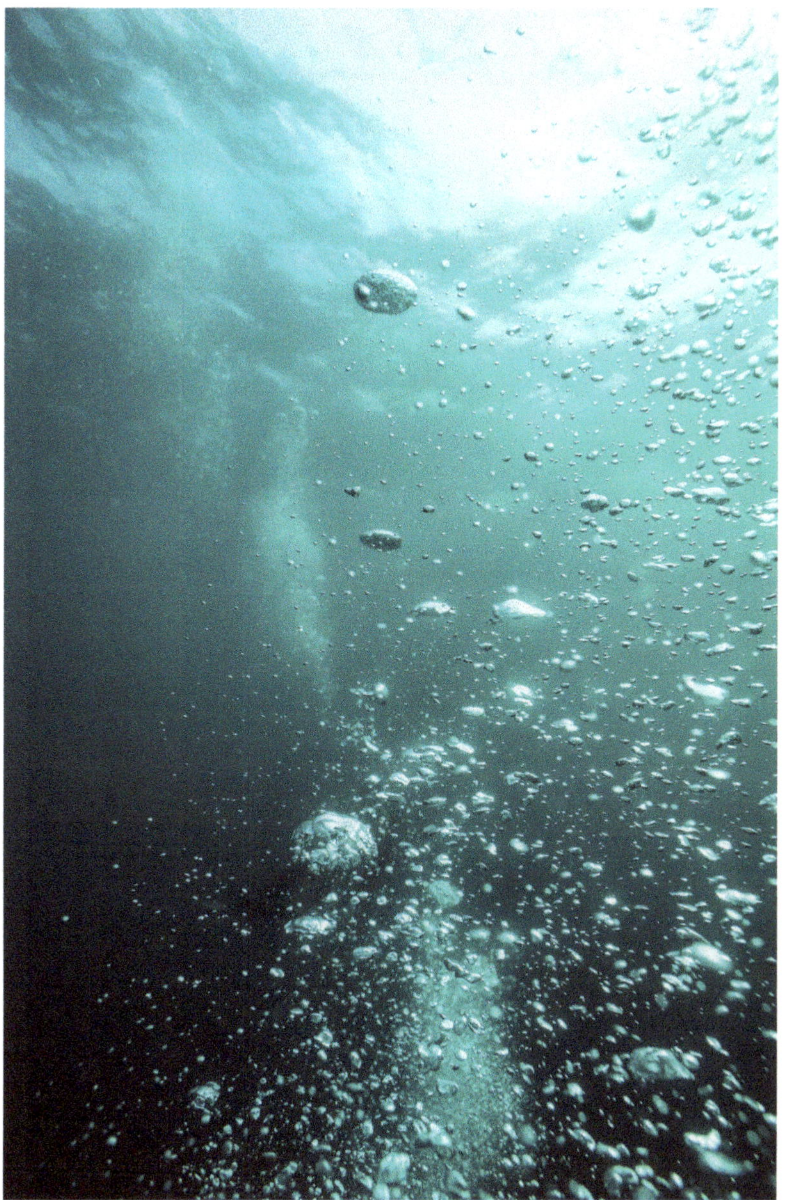

Naga, Näkki, and Suijin, form a safety shield around her—

this cortege of dreamers ushers her

through midnight-blue lake chambers,

where her hair ebbs and flows

and she remembers all her visions.

Her voice bubbles float,

sobbing through cerulean waves.

Kindred water spirits—Nixie, Ondine, Mami Wata

join the chorus echoing her ache.

They can see through her bony ribs,

to a diluted faint-red heart, and can understand

that even though she is *almost* a water sprite,

she longs to be back on recognizable shore,

combing.

Pierre's Sonnet

—inspired by Pierre Bonnard's Nude in Bathtub, c. 1940 – 46

Oh, Marthe, my muse, you are my favorite composition,
floating in the tub, performing your toilette
I sketch you first with hardly any third dimension,
then flood your limbs with aquarelle violet

Our dachshund, Poucette, lies happily nearby your bath
on blue hexagon floor-tiles that morph across the scene
The corner wall surrounds you with rectangle swatches
that shift as light turns blue to orange, yellow to green

Your left leg écru, your right one mauve, brown creases for
waist and bellybutton. Rarely do I give you facial
definition,
but I know everything about you intimately. I adore
your every stance, your daily tasks, your pale expression

My brushes tremble to find this was your final bath
Tuberculosis slaughtered your hues, a colorless aftermath

Caravaggio, A Story in Tenebroso

—inspired by Michelangelo da Caravaggio's painting
Beheading of Saint John the Baptist, 1608

Caravaggio, hailed as
genius painter, master of
chiaroscuro, was

also known as petty thief,
street brawler, suspected
murderer

A self-portrait within a
painting— there he is
in his jail cell,

peering toward his
subject, John the Baptist,
nearly dead, throat slit

Four characters standing
around play roles,
all luminous against

a murky background,
dun walls haloed by
an umber stone arch

A girl holds the golden
bowl for John's head,
a heartsick woman bows

The stern enforcer's
floodlit finger points
to command the final cut

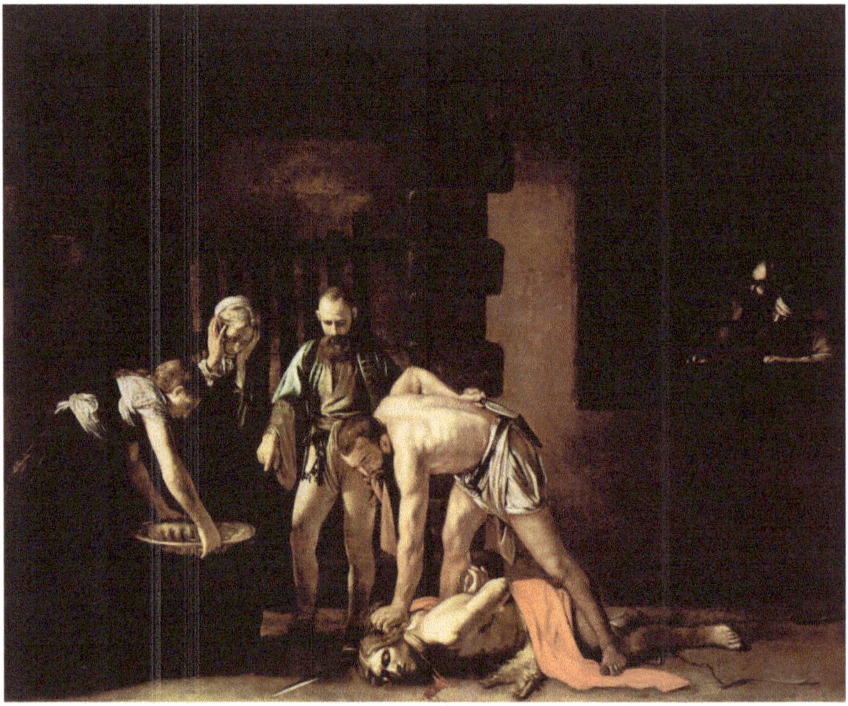

Designated slayer waits,
glistening knife hidden
behind his back,

ready to make the
severing slice, to pool
more oxblood on the cement

Caravaggio confesses
through drama of color, *he's*
John himself in fiery shroud

Violent, always in danger,
with his legacy brilliant,
mental state tenuous

His final paintings,
a self-imposed judgment
forecast his demise,

for his enemies were ready
with lead poisoning and blades,
planning a bloody vendetta

Dvořák Dreams

—after Refik Anadol's immersive artwork,
presented outside at the John F. Kennedy
Center, September 2024. *Dvořák Dreams*
blends contemporary art and music, using
AI algorithms to interpret Dvořák's melodies,
harmonies and rhythms

Visitors sit on
a grassy hill,
swirling colors flow
up and down
a thirty-two-foot high
screen.
Insistent rhythms pound
the courtyard,
even the willows
nearby sway, dance.

Impossible
to look away,
impossible not
to stamp the beat.

Will Dvořák appear?
A wave of pink, blue,
orange wriggles,
little pebbles
dot the waves,
nothing stops moving
or dancing.

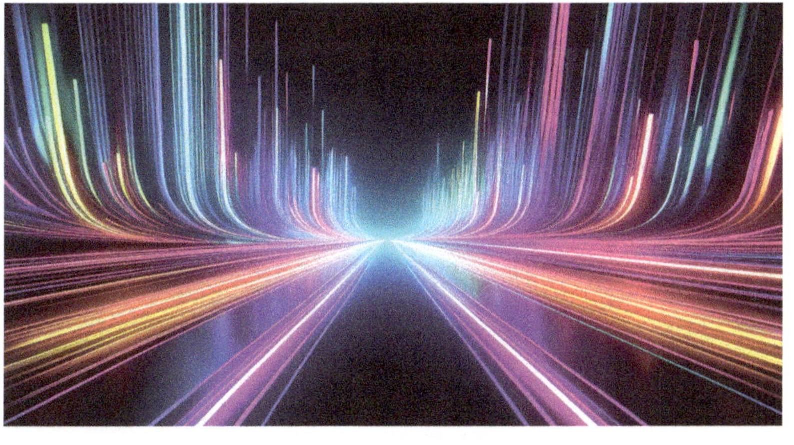

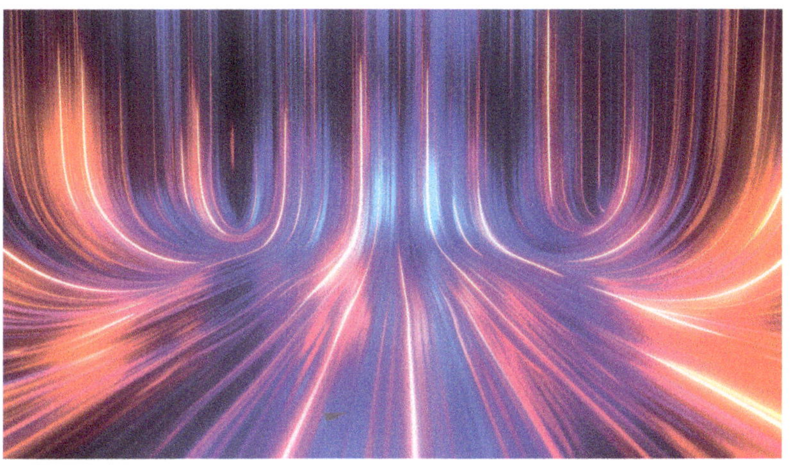

Impossible
to look away,
impossible not
to stamp the beat.
Our eyes and ears
must morph as well

We're underwater
with orange corals,
a city pops through,
a rhinoceros
lumbers across.
A city with a waterfront,
Statue of Liberty appears,
And now he's here!

Dvořák
twisting his whiskers,
conducting through
time.
The maestro revisits
Slavonic dances,
a strong downbeat,
with flute interlude.

African American
spirituals creep in,
weeping violins,
blaring French horns,
the dancing never dies.

Red, yellow, brown
billow once more,
tentacles and floppy
sea creatures slide
across.

Dvořák beckons

Impossible
to look away,
impossible not
to stamp the beat—
And, the drums, the drums
the drums.

Castles in the Air

Make a blueprint of your dreams. Ready?

Sketch your palace on cream vellum paper, 100 lb. stock.
Give it the title *Newcastle* using your best handwriting.
Fold the page in thirds, shrink it to a miniature size,
and seal it in a teeny mother-of-pearl box.
Wrap a 3-D printer in pink tissue tied with lavender ribbon.
Render that tiny too.

Cast a spell to lift you to the stars.

Wear a purple velvet jacket with side
pockets. Pack the miniature printer in the left one,
the mother-of-pearl box in the right. Strap a fanny
pack filled with dainty silver trophies around your tummy.
Rest horizontal on your pale aqua blanket
stuffed with soft cotton. Inhale. Exhale forever.

Whisper your mantra: Rise, rise, rise.

Float up through layers and layers of stratosphere,
memorize names of delicious colors as you drift by:
Hazelnut taupe, cabernet raisin, plum flan—
Choose *pêche-abricot* and slide in for a landing.
Plot on beaming up favorite friends and
invite them to Design Their Castle in the Sky.

They'll be wearing purple velvet jackets
carrying satchels of paint chips and mica.
Unpack your printer and diagram your doodles,
upload fanciful drawings into their minds.
Give gifts of amulets and trophies to spur magical ideas,
serve dulce de leche in mint-julep cups.

Introduce fantastic features—
Pietra dura walls of jewels,
beryl, garnet, peridot.

Balustrades of marbled mauve,
windows, arched and tall, a drawbridge—
There are no rules of architecture for castles
in the air. Leave your mark for hope, beauty.

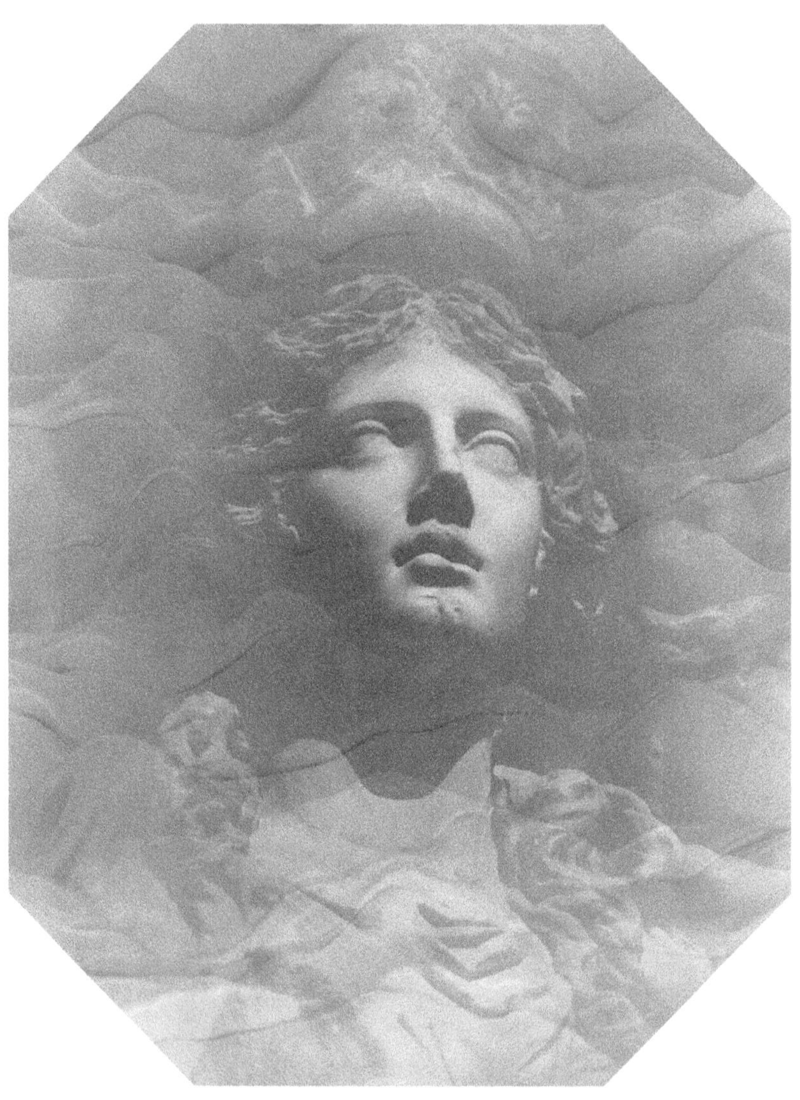

My Dinner with Athena

*—Greek myths tell us that Athena and Poseidon were arch
opponents for the right to be patron deity of Athens.*

She enters in gossamer white, aqua shawl
A huge golden pendant resembling an owl

She lays down her sword, puts it under the table
tosses her ringlets, fingers her sable

I start with some questions, she stops to confer
Can our waiter bring sea bass with olives for her?

He nods yes of course, his voice very low
Says our wine is divine, we should try Orvieto

Interrupted by flagrant toasts to her gardens,
And then by her boasts of sculptures, tall fountains

I start to forget why I wanted a mentor
She blithely neglected the reason we met here

So, I have to endure long tales of her party,
which she held in plein air, right next to the priory

Barbequed lamb, golden flames burning brightly
Her fans all brought gifts; they know she's quite arty

She relished the game of putting that guy down—
the one with the cloak, sharp trident upturned

Both were aware of their upcoming skirmish
Wily and fearless, she knew she would vanquish

I stop her mid-story, as I scream, "Please Athena!"
I need you to focus! Pay attention to me

Tell me how did we get here? Pray, what do you know?
She takes a small sip, hazel eyes start to glow—

Then she chants: *Life is dangerous, thrilling and glorious*
Work hard in your fields, don't make it laborious

Spin marvelous magic, be tough and ambitious
Keep reading, keep reading, be slyly capricious

Help all of your babies, give parties for friends
Do magnificent deeds!

And that was the end

She never explained the way we all got here
She was late for a séance, and readied to go

Floated up to the spot where her entourage waited
Climbed into the carriage and wrote on a scroll

I think she recorded a thought from our meeting
Silver ink— perhaps it was something I said?

She waved from her chariot, looking resplendent,
and murmured a blessing that I found transcendent:

May the gods be with you!

Mystic Color

—inspired by Hilma Af Klint's "Dove #1" from the series
Paintings for the Temple. Af Klint (1862–1944) made
hundreds of paintings, wrote hundreds of notebooks, and
designed a spiral museum for her major works, long before
the Guggenheim was built in 1937. Former poet laureate,
Joy Harjo, says of Af Klint, "She is intuitive and grounded in
the real world, with utter earthiness, but with sky knowledge."

I know what a human being is—I'm clairvoyant.

I show what a human being is through color—

a white/pink heart within a pink/white circle

on a light and dark rectangle split by a double helix.

When it comes to gender, pastel blue means female,

a soft milky yellow denotes male, the glow

of pink expresses love.

Born in 1862, I exist in the present—

when alive, I belonged in the future.

A resolute woman, during conventional times,

I was part of "The Five" who confirmed

through séance that there was a new way in art,

a new type of religion, a new way of being—

theosophy, trance, spiritual ecstasy.

The invisible "High Masters" directed me

to paint as my mind would lead me—

abstract design flowed through my hands.

They said the huge artworks would be

shown in "The Temple," a symbol

of eternal home, yet I pictured a spiral museum.

How mythical, how spectacular to be

guided by a force—my "Life's Work"

was compelled to be different, impregnated

by symbols—

Schooled in botanical drawing and

portraiture, I moved toward a different

geometric visual language—

my "poems of paint" become grids, circles,

spirals of abstraction, letters and words.

Before and after, then and now,

I am untethered to the recognizable world,

unlimited by real time.

I ricochet between extremes— ups and downs,

goods and evils, daydreams and nightmares—

black arcs, yellow ovals, kite-like sprays

of russet, cobalt blue, pale gray—punctuation

on lightly washed watercolor canvasses.

I slide around a prism, I confound, I reveal—

I exist and persist in a journey past the physical

for I know what a human being is.

Silver Is More than a Color

I am Silver. Who are you?
Are you intuitive and insightful too?

I am Silver, symbol of purity
A precious ore of color that's sparkly

Included in the broad family of whites
At heart, I'm introspective and bright

Not a dull shade of *gray* like platinum,
nor am I gunmetal, chrome, or aluminum

A gleaming element when added to oil,
I help artists to reflect light like foil

My versatility is prized in technology,
used in touch screens, circuits, and dentistry

An anti-microbial, I fight infection
Worn as a bracelet, aid flu prevention

I am Silver, feminine in quality,
aligned with the moon, a celestial body

I am Silver, refined and sleek,
the color of grace, a hint of mystique

I am Silver, ductile and malleable,
willing to change, soft and flexible

I am a metal with flair and fortitude
I'm more than a color,

Call me attitude!

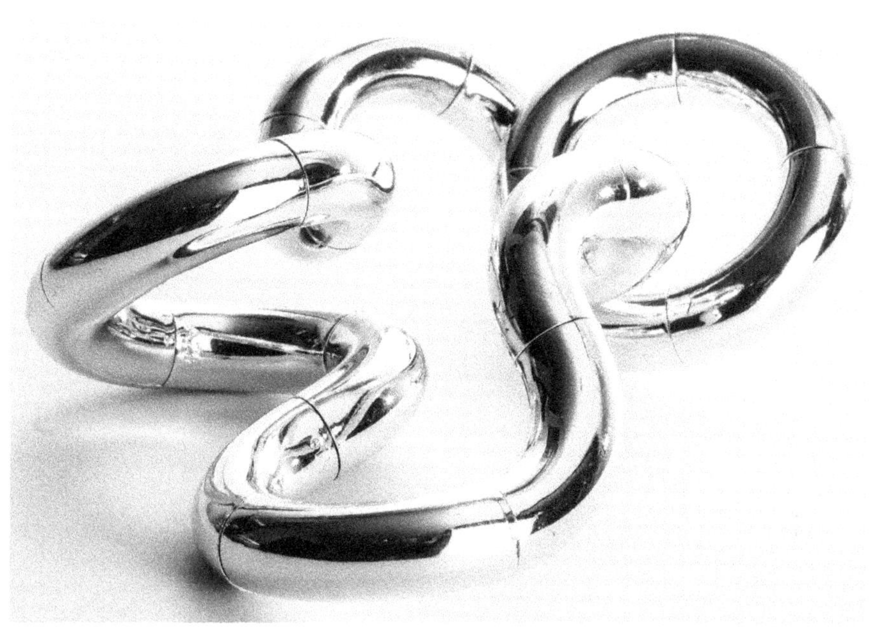

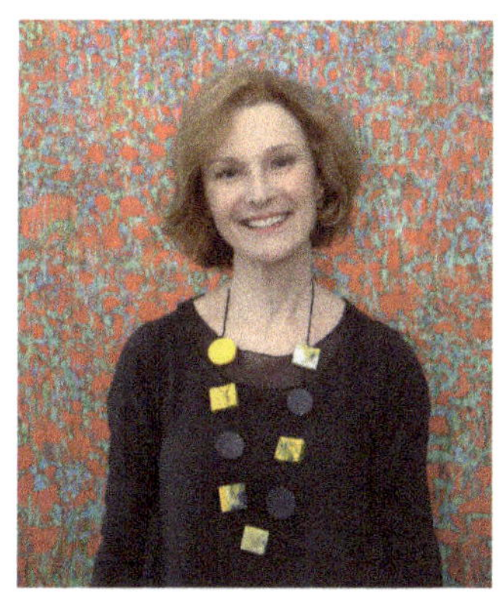

photo: Sonya Melescu

LEE WOODMAN is the author of the *"Scapes"* poetry series (*Homescapes, Mindscapes, Lifescapes, Artscapes,* and *Soulscapes*) and winner of the Independent Press Gold Award 2025, the Nautilus Gold Award for Poetry 2025, and the Independent Press Award for Distinguished Favorite in Poetry 2023. She is also winner of the 2020 William Meredith Prize for Poetry, the 2021 Atlantic Review International Poetry Competition Merit Award, and First Prize in Poetry and Prose Contest for Carve Magazine 2022.

Her essays and poems have been published in *Poet Lore, Tiferet Journal, Zócalo Public Square, Grey Sparrow Press, The Ekphrastic Review, vox poetica, The New Guard Review, The Concord Monitor, The Hill Rag, Naugatuck River Review, Tulip Tree Publishing,* and *The Broadkill Review.* A Pushcart nominee, she received an Individual Poetry Fellowship from the DC Commission on the Arts and Humanities FY 2019 and FY 2020, and a Virginia Center for the Creative Arts Fellowship in 2022. Woodman has been a featured guest on numerous radio shows and podcasts, including Grace Cavalieri's *Poet and the Poem* at the Library of Congress, *The Packaged Tourist Show* at The National Archives with Andrew Dibiase, *The Authors Show* with Don McCauley, and *Gab Talks* with Gabby Olczak.

Shanti Arts

Nature • Art • Spirit

Please visit us online
to browse our entire book catalog,
including poetry collections and fiction,
books on travel, nature, healing, art,
photography, and more.

Also take a look at our highly regarded art
and literary journal, *Still Point Arts Quarterly*,
which may be downloaded for free.

www.shantiarts.com

www.ingramcontent.com/pod-product-compliance
Lightning Source LLC
Chambersburg PA
CBHW050031040726
47599CB00015B/1630